Peter —
I hope these travels
through history
let you see the world
in a new way.
Best
[signature]
10/22/97

When People Could Fly

Books by Morton Marcus

Origins (Kayak, 1969)
Where the Oceans Cover Us (Capra, 1972)
The Santa Cruz Mountain Poems (Capra, 1972)
The Armies Encamped in the Fields Beyond the Unfinished Avenues:
       Prose Poems (Jazz Press, 1977)
Big Winds, Glass Mornings, Shadows Cast by Stars:
       Poems, 1972-1980 (Jazz Press, 1980)
The Brezhnev Memo (Dell/Delacorte, 1981) {Novel}
Pages From a Scrapbook of Immigrants (Coffee House, 1988)

When People Could Fly

Morton Marcus

Hanging Loose Press
Brooklyn, New York

Published by Hanging Loose Press, 231 Wyckoff Street, Brooklyn, New York 11217. All rights reserved. No part of this book may be reproduced without the publisher's written permission, except for brief quotations in reviews.

Printed in the United States of America
10 9 8 7 6 5 4 3 2 1

Many of these pieces first appeared, in slightly different forms, in the following publications: *Alcatraz, Asylum Annual* (issues 1994 & 1995), *The Barnabe Mountain Review* (#1, 2, 3), *Caliban, The Denver Quarterly, The Exquisite Corpse, Fiction* (#12/2 & 14/2), *Hanging Loose* (#68 & 70), *Kayak, Key Satch(el)* (#1,2,4,5), *Melting Trees* (#1,2,3,4,6), *The Montserrat Review* (#1 & 2), *Pares Cum Paribus: Autor de la Semana* (Chile), *The Porter Gulch Review, The Prose Poem: An International Journal* (#2,3,4,5,6), *The World*, and in the following anthologies: *A Curious Architecture: Contemporary British and American Prose Poems* (England, 1996), *The Party Train: North American Prose Poetry* (1996), and *American Poets Say Goodbye to the 20th Century* (1996). "The Story That Had Never Been Written" and "The Novel" were originally broadcast on National Public Radio's *The Sound of Writing*.

Special thanks to my daughter, Jana Marcus, for her love and her unending hours of work on this manuscript, and to Michael Catalano, Gerald Fleming, and Peter Johnson for their encouragement and for publishing a number of these pieces in their journals.

Hanging Loose Press wishes to thank the Literature Program of the New York State Council on the Arts for a grant in support of this book's publication.

Cover art: *Song of the Shepherd* by James Carl Aschbacher
Cover design: Caroline Drabik

Library of Congress Cataloging-in-Publication Data

Marcus, Morton
    When people could fly / Morton Marcus.
      p. cm.
    ISBN 1-882413-45-8 (cloth). -- ISBN 1-882413-44-X (pbk.)
    I. Title.
PS3563.A639W48   1997
811'.54--dc21   97-29674
                           CIP

Produced at The Print Center, Inc., 225 Varick St., New York, NY 10014, a non-profit facility for literary and arts-related publications. (212) 206-8465

CONTENTS

When People Could Fly

The Manual for Twentieth-Century Man (and Woman)

Journeys

To Donna
for her humanity,
integrity,
wisdom,
and especially
her love

Death and life were not
Till man made up the whole,
Made lock, stock and barrel
Out of his bitter soul,
Aye, sun and moon and star, all,
And further add to that
That, being dead, we rise,
Dream and so create
Translunar Paradise.
I have prepared my peace
With learned Italian things
And the proud stones of Greece,
Poet's imaginings
And memories of love,
Memories of the words of women,
All those things whereof
Man makes a superhuman
Mirror-resembling dream.

W.B.Yeats

When People Could Fly

The Big Broadcast

The universe lacks clarity. The edges of things scatter, explosions of light reaching out in sparks, filaments, threads that fray into the future of something else.

Knowledge is sequence, not tense, and in that sense space, not time, is ticking in our heads, matter is all that matters and nothing is the matter with that.

What is immortal in us is not moral but those feelers of light merging with the next object we touch, those antennae surrounding us like radiant body hairs that sipped from something else that sipped from us whatever, at that instant, we were.

The sound of the universe is not static, but sucking and slurping, each form passing on the message that needs no decoding because it is encoded in every thing: you eat me and I eat you, a light meal arriving from the kitchen of the sun.

The radio signals from deep space broadcast soap operas, *crimes passionels*, injustices, private and public scandals more (or less) lurid than those we devise because they are us:

She loved him and he did or did not love her, God's radiant lips appearing out of the eternal dark to thunder against each other like a celestial radio announcer's, telling us to tune in, not out, same time, same place, because the universe, more quarky than quirky, will be continued.

Mathematics

The number 1 wanders alone in his short-brimmed cap at the edge of the sunlit field. I love him because he is pure, because he is all ego and all beginning, because he concentrates on himself and all first causes, in perpetual solitude: the one sun, the one field; the one tree, ant, squirrel; the one bobcat. One is the archetype of archetypes, the soul of souls struggling to comprehend the soul of the tree, the essence of the bobcat. No wonder he is the namer of plants and animals.

And I am overjoyed with the number 2; its long swan neck entrances me. It is exotic in the same way anything encountered for the first time is exotic. But it provides an even greater pleasure because it is the other side of 1, the part he could not see but always knew was there—the part suggested by his shadow. 2 is the night sky to one's daylit field. 2 is the coupling of two ones, the merging of two solitudes, the second of two eyes which allows the head to see two realities, the realities of the right and the left sides.

But I am more excited by the infant shape of 3 than by the shapes of 1 and 2 put together. Can that be? Yes, because 3 is the child of the first two, the combination of both, the offspring beyond their egos. It plays in the field of its father, it reaches for the stars of its mother.

All progressions proceed from the number 3.

The First Game

The first game was Adam naming the animals. It was also the first time God and Adam had something to talk about.

As God led each animal before Adam in that topiaried silence of eternal foliage and crystalline breezes, Adam pronounced any sound that came into his still-empty mind.

"Rhinoceros!" Adam said and snorted and whinnied his unrestrained delight at the sound the word made in the air, while God chuckled.

"Pelican!" And both God and Adam laughed aloud, as the bird waddled out of nothingness, flexing its wings and shaking its head.

"Girrrrrraffe!" Adam squeezed out, attempting to express in sound the elongated neck bobbing past the topmost leaves of the yet-to-be-named tree in front of him. And both he and God laughed some more.

Each word took wing in the silence, flailing or gliding, floundering to the ground where it crawled under a bush, or settling on a branch where it looked down expectantly at the two beings, as if waiting to be called.

Soon the pristine air was heavy with the presence of words, crowded with meanings.

And all the while, God and Adam continued to laugh, staggering under the trees, each with an arm around the other's shoulders.

"Wart hog!" And what was now a wart hog trotted past.

"Mosquito!" And a flake of light, no larger than a dust mote, whizzed by their heads.

"Ostrich!"

And through his laughter, God slapped Adam on the back, exclaiming, "This is more fun than a barrel of—"

"Monkeys!" Adam yelled, as a quartet of chimpanzees scampered and somersaulted past them.

And God and Adam laughed together from sunrise to sunset, laughed deep into the night, laughed and laughed until the tears came.

Gravity

Once people laughed all the time. That was long ago, when the earth was nothing but nailed together layers of rock littered with the broken dishes God's mother had thrown from the windows of her new house. In those days there existed a breed of sheep whose hooves were like the claws on hammers. Wherever these sheep stepped, they pulled up the nails that held the earth together, and stones and boulders would float up behind them, and the planet sway.

When adults or children saw a rock drifting toward the sky, they would lunge for it, wrestle it into the crevice it had come from, and holding it there with one hand, they would yank from their cummerbunds the nails and hammer they always carried, and pound the rock into place.

Constantly looking for such floating material, manufacturing nails and hammers, and tending the sheep were the principal occupations in those days.

Still, the people laughed all the time and loved the hammer-clawed sheep. They used the sheep's wool for clothing, blankets and the walls of their tents, and reluctantly ate the sheep for food, reasoning that everything had its drawbacks, whatever they might be. Take the crockery-strewn landscape: the people would have been overjoyed for one or two trees.

The people prized the sheep for their loving dispositions. Even wild ones would wander up and nuzzle a group of humans sitting around a campfire, many times settling down next to them when one of the old shepherds told the story of how God, after he had made good, built the new house for his mother, or how the stars were lanterns belonging to a restless tribe of wonderers who had wandered into the sky, taking all the light with them, which, by agreement with the tribes who remained behind, they used in their lanterns only half the day.

The stories served as reminders of how all things were connected, and made the people, chuckling respectfully, cherish the sheep all the more.

And then there were the sheep's voices, so soft and mild they soothed the listeners' most distressing thoughts, relaxing their muscles, and making their smiles widen.

But life was too hard: the scraggly bushes and dusty cabbages, the children cutting themselves on the broken dishes or twisting their ankles as they ran after the floating rocks—things had to change.

And so the prayers began, and the older shepherds were soon making deals with angels while everyone slept, until one day the people woke to find the sheep gone, the rocks in place, the dishes swept up, and very little to smile about.

Within a day, there were patches of greenery; and a week later, slender saplings; and before the month was out, wooly green trees with singing birds inside them, which everyone agreed wasn't the same as the voices of the sheep or their nuzzling presence. But the elders halted all criticism by insisting that "under the circumstances" this was the best deal they could get.

Most trying of all, especially to the children, was the attitude of the rocks. Not only did they no longer float about; they burrowed into the soil as if they had turned away from the sunlight and yearned to be underground. This made the people sadder than they already were, and a delegation went to the old shepherds to complain.

"This is what you wanted us to do," the elders replied. "Soon there will be flowers and gardens, vegetables and fruits. But the laughter is gone forever. We traded it for gravity which keeps the rocks in place but also keeps you from laughing. It was one or the other. You could have remained connected and had nothing, or become separate and have the fruits of the earth. Thus you have chosen. Thus it shall be."

The people turned back to their tents with tears in their eyes, even as the grass spread far and wide over the rocks and the red and yellow flowers unfurled everywhere in the landscape.

And God saw that it was not good and took pity on his people, and came to the eldest shepherd in a dream. "Behold, I am not a cruel god," he said. "Look at the new house I built for my mother. Let my people know that I will allow them to break their gravity with laughter and singing from time to time, and although the sheep will not return, I will simulate their voices in everyone's heart through the words of certain men and women, henceforth to be known as poets, so my people should not always be sad but at the same time should never forget what they, through their folly, have lost."

The People We Never Heard Of

Where did they go, the people we never heard of?

Did they build those sandstone monuments that slump in the desert or crumble in the tightening web of jungle vines?

Not the Egyptians or Mayans or the people who inhabited Angkor Wat, but the ones we never heard of, who came like a wind through the passes, fluttered into this valley or that, and were gone, leaving humps in the land, maybe a rock formation here and there, and utensils whose markings we cannot decipher.

If matter can neither be created nor destroyed, the people we never heard of are still here, just over that hill, where we can't see them, or behind our eyes, where their presence is a pressure we intuit more than understand.

I mean, do we lift a spoon, tie a knot, smile and weep as we do because those people did it first, showing us how?

A thousand years from now when this planet is a single city and the oceans are ponds in a system of municipal parks, will our descendants come across our markings for trees and whales, unable to decipher them, and sense a pressure building behind their eyes and a longing rolling through their chests for things they no longer have words for, things irrevocably gone?

The Oceans

Don't remind me that we resemble the seas, that we are 67% water, and that the taste of our tears is salt from the ocean deeps.

I want to forget those vast uncertainties that go on doing what they do each day, year after year, unable to find any peace.

Their restlessness unnerves me. Their frustrated rages incite my own, as they shift one way and another, shaking their fists at the stars, going nowhere, stuck to the depressions of the planet from which they cannot escape.

And yet I do not look forward to the day when the oceans will rise up and wrench themselves free, dragging all our memories with them.

In a dream once I saw the oceans surging and tumbling through space, stretching and contracting into any shape they could imagine, sporting like a school of dolphin, as they experienced for the first time the joy of being whatever they wanted to be.

In their excitement, however, they forgot where they were, and looking over their shoulders they searched for that cinder which for eons they had considered, for want of a better name, home.

But the cinder was no longer there. At the oceans' departure, it had continued spinning in the opposite direction, so the location the oceans sought was a calculation that pinpointed empty space.

Now the oceans existed in an endless moment, a continuous vacancy that extended in all directions, and it made no difference where they moved or how they moved there.

Soon they began to founder and roll, tentatively feeling with their edges for any kind of landfall.

Finally, they were shapeless masses, without sound or meaning, unable to cry out the immense longings they contained for imprisoning shorelines and lost tides.

The Duke, the Demon, and the Sacred Grove

for George Ow, Jr.

The duke of Jin dreamt that a demon with hair of fire and lumpy, boil-strewn skin smashed through the palace gates and the doors of the inner apartments and stood at the foot of his bed, howling for vengeance.

"What does this mean?" the duke asked the sorcerer of the Bamboo Grove the next morning.

"Your highness will not live to eat the new grain," the old man replied.

Three months later, the duke summoned the sorcerer to attend him at a banquet, a ceremonial occasion featuring buns made from the grain the duke had levied as taxes on the latest harvest. "Your error has cost you your life," he said to the old man, nodding to a guard, who decapitated the sorcerer on the spot.

No sooner had the duke swallowed the first bun, however, than his stomach swelled from the grain and he fell dead.

The story concludes with a middle-aged servant who the night before, huddling in a stable and shivering from cold, had dreamt that he was carrying the duke to heaven on his back. Because of this dream, he is the one ordered to haul the duke's body from the banquet table to the mortuary, and is then beheaded so his spirit can accompany the duke's on its heavenly journey.

I always confuse this story with another from the same book. In the second tale, a brash young man challenges the Sacred Grove to a game of dice, wagering his life against the use of the Grove's resident genie. He tosses the dice for the Grove and himself and wins, but the Grove, which has said nothing to the young man from the start, will not give up its Spirit and, despite this ecologically symbolic stance, rots and dies within the week.

My confusion begins when I look up the second story in the book, *The Zou Zhuan and Other Classics of Early Chinese History*, and find that the tale I remembered is not the one there. It turns out that for some unknown reason the Grove *has* consented to the wager, lends its Spirit to the young man as agreed, but dies because the young man refuses to return the Spirit at the appointed time.

This version is certainly more plausible and ecologically suggestive than mine, but within a day I am again confusing the story in the book with the one I imagined. Add to this the notion I got from heaven knows where that the demon of the duke's dream is really the Spirit of the Sacred Grove gone berserk because he could no longer find his home, that the sorcerer of the Bamboo Grove is the brash young man grown old, and that the grain which swells the duke's stomach is a seed that contains the beginnings of a new Sacred Grove but was snatched from the genie's hand as he was about to plant it—and it is clear that somewhere in my psyche the genie howls vengeance at the foot of the duke's bed because he envisions the duke three months later devouring the future he has been robbed of in the past.

I guess joining the two tales together and extrapolating from them fulfills a need in me that insists on creating order from chaos, so that my confusing the stories, in the end, is a way of making everything clear. Everything, that is, except the servant who dreamt the wrong dream at the wrong time. Unless, of course, poor, in rags, needing to pay a compulsory state tax he could not afford, the servant is the one who snatched the seed from the genie's hand as he was about to plant it.

The Sorcerer's Apprentice

Tiresias is sitting in the doorway of his hut, his skirts hiked up showing his withered inner thighs, as he stares at the town below with sightless eyes.

He has just been told by his page, the boy who leads him, who cooks for him and washes his clothes, who bathes and oils his wrinkled reptilian skin, that the queen is dead and the young king, after stabbing out his eyes, has been led away in misery and ruin; that everything he told the king two hours before has come to pass.

The old man shuffles his sandals in the dust. The boy sees no pleasure in his face. The quarrelsome prophet, whose feisty frame shook with anger at the king a short time before, does not look satisfied. Like the universe, he is expressionless and blind.

Bending forward on his golden staff, the old man looks as if he's peering into the future, but the boy knows that is only the way the old rise or remain steady even when they sit, leaning their weight on anything that will hold them up.

If the old man sees anything, the boy thinks, it is the last thing he ever saw. Out hunting on Helicon as a youth no older than the boy is now, he came thirsty to the spring around a hill, and found the goddess naked, bathing there, her body so dazzling its reflection was sunlight glancing off the water and shattering like glass in both his eyes.

That was not her punishment, but the Law's: to see the unseeable, the boy knows, is to lose one's sight. In compensation, the goddess gave the old man inner vision, declaring him prophet with the power to speak with birds, and handed him the staff he leans on now to guide him through his darkened days.

What the boy cannot perceive is what the old man thinks; that knowing is the curse that gives the prophet such little pleasure he can no longer force a single expression to flutter across his bony face.

The prophet knew Oedipus's fate years ago, saw behind his clouded eyes the queen, Oedipus's wife and mother, swinging in a noose above her bed even before the child was born. In the same way, he sees himself years from now in the land of the dead, enticed through dim caverns to drink from the pit of blood Odysseus will prepare in order to learn from him the way home.

The way home. Why is it always that and not the other, more pertinent question: whether the life at home will warrant the hardships of the journey. Home for Oedipus was horror, was husbanding his mother and murdering his father. It is the place from which he has been driven now, a wanderer once again, knowing but sightless, cursed as he, the aged prophet, all these years has been. The boredom Odysseus will find at home will be no better.

The old man sits back, letting the staff fall against his shoulder like the great oar he will tell Odysseus to bring into the land where men are ignorant of the sea. Useless advice, always useless: to know the future but to be unable to change it. That's the knowledge that sears his inner sight, just as his vision of the goddess had scorched his eyeballs and burned his optic nerves like candle wicks.

The boy knows none of this. He watches the old man lift the staff from his shoulder with both hands and, as he has done so many times before, tease the dust before him with its tip. Sometimes the prophet absently sketches pictures in the dust, or traces words whose esoteric meanings only the birds can understand, and his face, expressionless as always, will be lost somewhere beyond his body and the world.

At such times, the boy who leads him, who cooks for him and washes his clothes, who bathes and rubs his reptilian skin with fragrant oils, watches fascinated, silently moving his lips as he memorizes the words and imitates the old man's drawings with a slender twig, scratching in the dirt those symbols he doesn't comprehend. Once he scrapes the twig against the ground, he is unable to stop, although he is shaken with nausea and becomes deliriously ill, while the stick—he's sworn to several friends—trembles in his hand like a snake about to awaken from a trance.

The True Cross

for Clem Starck

We never ask if, as carpenter, he thought about the proportions and notched connections, or how well the wood was planed and the pieces fit, when he first grasped the rough cross. Remember, he had the trained eye, the professional's ability to estimate shoddy work or work well done. Did he, for a moment, want to redo or improve that instrument of his death?

I ask this in all seriousness. The True Cross scraped against his fingertips and palms, maybe catching on calluses and cuts, maybe resting on the grooved lifeline that was about to run out, and I imagine he must have been more engrossed by those shreds of experience than by any notions of resurrection or everlasting life.

The iron nails that slammed through his palms and attached him to the wood, glancing off bone and shattering knuckles, had to be large enough to support the weight of a man, let alone a god. Did he appreciate the bureaucratic thoroughness that had taken into consideration even that?

The man who built the True Cross must have risen before dawn in the chilly blue light, and maybe grumbled that he had to make three crosses before nine that morning. Possibly his wife called to him as he left the hut to remind him of their visit to her parents' house that evening, or to ask him for a few dinars to buy cloth that afternoon in the marketplace, where, she said, she planned to go, unless the crowds were too large because of the executions announced for later in the day.

Three Lost Tales of the
Baal Shem Tov

Who has not heard of the Baal Shem Tov? Each of his tales is a leaf on the tree of his legend, the tree that shines like a shaft of flame in the shadowy garden of our imagination.

★

"Forget about how many angels dance on the point of a pin, or how many souls can slide through the eye of a needle. Those problems are the syllogisms of tailors," he said. "The only question worth asking is whether the dead push us from the earth through the tree, so they can fly once more from the wings of the leaves, or whether we're dragged upwards from the stones until like birds we sing the praises of God from the highest branches."

When asked in Berditchev whether he thought we were shoved from below or tugged from above, he answered, "From above. It's God's way of glorifying the dead."

Another time, in Kamenetz, he answered, "From below. It's the dead's way of glorifying us."

However, in Horodenko he replied to a feeble old man leaning on his grandson, "Both. It's God's way of glorifying the dead and their way of glorifying us."

But when he was asked this same question in Sadigor by a drayman whose wife had recently died, he said, "Neither. What makes you think our lives are dependent on the whims of God or the dead, and have nothing to do with us?"

"How can this be!" cried Reb Tzvi-Hersh Sofier, the Baal Shem's life-long scribe, as the crowd in the Sadigor marketplace stood astonished. "Two years ago you answered, 'From above.' Last year, 'From below.' Two months ago, 'Both.' And now, 'None of the three.'"

The Baal Shem turned to his scribe, nodded toward the drayman's sad eyes and dishevelled clothes, and said, shaking his head, "Tzvi, Tzvi!"

Later that day when they were walking alone on the road to Polnoye, the frustrated scribe trotted around his master and continued to upbraid him. "How could you say that God determines our lives in one place, that the dead do in another, that both do in a third, and that we do in a fourth?"

The master shrugged. "Tzvi, you never look to see whom I am talking to. For each of the four there was a correct answer that wasn't correct for the others. Besides, I'm sure you think that at least one of the answers was right, so why quibble?"

★

Clapping his hands, a disciple of the Baal Shem leaped up from the prayer table, beaming. "I've just discovered men and women's most important secret: they love God, whether they know it or not."

The Baal Shem looked up from a letter he had just received, and nodded. "Good. Now you have to learn God's most important secret with equal conviction."

"What's that?" asked the disciple.

"Why," said the Baal Shem turning back to the letter, "that whether or not God knows it, He loves us."

★

This is what the Baal Shem Tov, the Master of the Holy Name, said to his disciples as they rested in a forest on the road to Lwow.

"I have told you how enraptured I was when I was alone in the mountains. I learned the language of stones and trees, of donkeys and sparrows, and I have told you how hard it was to come down into the towns and villages and live among people.

"But I have also told you that we must live among people, with their sorrows and pettiness, their transgressions and self-righteousness, no matter how much we yearn to remain with the wind of God's voice on the mountain tops.

"To live with people and help them is our duty. But we also have a duty to go into the mountains so we never lose touch with God's voice.

"Many of you have said that these two roles are a contradiction. But are they? There is the raindrop we see that taps the surface of the pond and makes the water shudder in all directions. That is our life among people and shows how each of our actions affects others.

"However, there is the raindrop we don't see that slips through the surface and disappears without a ripple, as if the surface had opened a tiny fish mouth, closed around the rain drop like a pearl, and swallowed it without leaving a trace. This is our life alone.

"Who is to say which raindrop is doing God's work and which is not? Both are part of a community of raindrops that are collectively called a pond, which at night luminously reflects the stars, many of which we recognize and many we do not, and some we do not even notice as they slide down the sky and disappear."

When People Could Fly

I

The flying phenomenon occurred for only a brief period in history and was marked, says biologist Isobel Simms in *Flight, the Great Secret*, "by the cells' ability to fill with oxygen and maintain it when a person took an exceptionally deep breath. Then with as little effort as passing to the brain the message to rise from a chair or walk, the individual sent the brain instructions to fly. At this command the body, visibly swollen, would rise from the ground with the portly grace of a hot air balloon."

The most serious problem confronting the flyers was wind, since sudden tugs of air, unexpected downdrafts, or long sweeps of horizontal gale-like currents could blow a person far from home. Most people, however, soon learned not to fly too high, and the majority achieved the required dexterity by utilizing the wind to their advantage through kicking, pawing or sailing on the air currents, or through using their hands and feet as rudders. As an added precaution, people avoided flying after dark and in bad weather, except in cases of emergency.

Like flight, landing was achieved by sending a message to the brain to descend, at which the cells slowly released the stored oxygen "in a sort of cellular decompression," says Simms, and the body drifted downward, feet first, touching the earth with virtually no impact, although children, to their parents' consternation, tried to "belly in" or "dive headfirst." The descent was so slow, however, that the result of such juvenile enthusiasms was almost always harmless.

II

This "evolutionary quirk," as nineteenth century biologist Jacques Hebert termed the flying phenomenon, lasted for roughly a hundred years, coming to prominence somewhere between 960 and 1020 A.D., a period of relative global tranquillity, when the Holy Roman Empire was revived in Europe, the Sung Dynasty was established in China, King Bagauda brought settled rule to Kano in Africa (where the Empire of Ghana was already in the middle of its 130-year Golden Age), the Mayans had come out of the jungle and were flourishing on the Yucatan Peninsula, and Mahmud, the Turkish ruler of Ghazni, founded his empire in North India.

At that time the earth was composed of a handful of large cities from which many roads led through forests and valleys, plains and mountain ranges, joining scattered towns and villages, which when seen from horseback or on foot appeared greatly isolated from each other, but when viewed from high above revealed themselves to be inextricably bound in an interlocking series of routes which webbed Europe, Asia and Africa in a continuous network of highways, roads and trails. There is no doubt that this latter picture must have been the one seen by people as they flew.

Historians such as Gaspar Rodriguez and Christopher Burne-Smith speculate that it was this changed point of view, in fact, which brought about the period of peace and harmony that prevailed over most of the planet at this time and, until the discovery of the flying documents, had been thought of as a coincidence or an "aberration in human relationships," as social anthropologist Willard Petry recently wrote.

III

How people discovered they could fly has still not been established, but by 980 A.D., designated town councils in Europe and Asia were regularly taking to the air at the least provocation. When factions within a village disagreed on a religious or political issue, or when two towns disputed a boundary or the behavior of their citizens in one another's territory, these councils would rise into the air over their respective clusters of houses, until each group was satisfied that the other was not armed. Then drifting toward one another and sitting cross-legged in one large assembly hundreds of feet above the countryside, these councils of the air would discuss their differences "through the sunlit mornings and afternoons," wrote Claude of Anjou, "as cloud-shadows dragged over the quilt-like landscape below."

Discovered in the archives of the Abbey of Toulouse in 1952, the private diary of this venerable historian, who lived from 950-1030 and is known chiefly for his work on the rise of the German Kingdom under Otto I, reveals Claude to have been an eye-witness to a number of these mid-air meetings, which at one point he describes to have been "as much heightened spiritually as they were physically, as if the bird's-eye view of the landscape below had struck the participants with a realization of the insignificance of their covetousness and complaints, although their closeness to God's canopy could also explain the almost always felicitous results of these convocations."

Entries in the long-suppressed 1000-volume Chinese encyclopedia, begun in 978 and confined to the use of only the most eminent scholars until the communist takeover in 1949, document a detailed picture of how similar meetings were carried out in that country. "The talks, rarely led by a government functionary, were conducted by representative village elders, whom all below could see discussing the issue, sitting crosslegged while bobbing on the air currents, the hems of their gowns rippling like pennants from their seated figures." Another entry concludes, "These harmonious pictures seem to have filled the peasantry with such serenity and good humor that they went about their business with happy hearts."

Similar reports have been found in histories written everywhere on the planet during this period, and where writing was unknown, such as in the New World and Africa, stone carvings on temples and steles depict the same observations in pictorial terms (see Carl Abbot, *The Mayan Steles Speak*, pp. 186-201).

IV

Psychiatrists as diverse in theory as Hans Klepmeyer and Shu-tung Wu agree that the attainment of height, even through mountain-climbing, when one can survey the landscape from a commanding vantage point, affects the psyche by relaxing dogmatic opinions and rigid adherences to belief systems, even when those systems occur within such core areas as religion and politics.

Both cite the ego's loss of self-importance when distanced by height from communal pressures, and both describe the period when people could fly, in Shu-tung's words "as probably the most serenely joyous in the history of the human psyche."

Conversely, in Klepmeyer's words, "We have seen the scale of viciousness to which petty concerns can give rise when people are forced to live on the same mental and physical level bound by rigidly grounded traditions— that is, when they cannot 'see' their problems from 'heightened' perspectives. Such unavoidably metaphoric language should not be dismissed as fanciful. Nor should we forget that such tyrannical world leaders as Napoleon and Hitler were 'short' or 'small' men in the several meanings of those words."

Both cite the "serenely joyous" aspect of flying with several examples from the travel diaries of the Russian merchant Sergei Rubikov, which show the evolution of the town council assemblies, especially in the Kingdom of Hungary, which had been established "with 46 counties and 10 dioceses under Stephen I in 955." Rubikov tells us, "Here various church–

men and court officials record that groups of the populace, through their own enterprise, organized spontaneous, or regularly scheduled, festivals of the air, where the peasantry of the different towns would hold feasts and pageants high above their villages for the inhabitants of neighboring townships. I saw with my own eyes how these festivals had grown into county celebrations complete with food stalls, games, sporting and musical events and demonstrations of local handicrafts."

In France, England, and the German states, the early guilds organized the festivals. In many cases several guilds joined together to present the event, which became the basis of a friendly rivalry, especially in Hamburg and Lubeck and other north German towns, where, medievalist Rudolph Kempe argues, such cooperation among the guilds was the impetus behind the formation of the Hanseatic League several hundred years later and, more recently, of the organization of the German soccer leagues.

Such speculations have fascinated historians and anthropologists in all parts of the world. Ethnographers in the United States, such as E. Forrest Taylor, for example, have sought to explain the origin of the Northwest Indian Potlatch in conjunction with the flying phenomenon, and cite the shaman whistles, spoon handles, and totem depictions of humans on the backs of various flying creatures as vestiges of tribal memories concerning incidents that occurred during this period.

V

When the first documents regarding human flight came to light in the eighteenth century, religious leaders of every belief claimed that their particular God had blessed believers with the power to fly. At the same time, historians were convinced that the phenomenon had occurred only in their own countries and proved the superiority of their race as well as their nation. But as more and more evidence appeared from around the planet, each with its own claim of religious, racial, and national superiority, these areas of study were quietly abandoned.

Other historians argued that only the economically or socially privileged classes had been able to fly. But this notion was abruptly curtailed by the explicit identification in the archival material of "the populace" or "the peasantry" as being the ones observed flying.

Similarly, most historians of the nineteenth century attempted to prove that only men had been able to fly, insisting that the inferiority of women, both physically and morally, argued against their inclusion in "the brotherhood of flight," as Nelson Thomas, one of these historians, wrote in 1876.

More subtle scholars speculated on the many mid-air accidents which would have been reported had women been given the power to fly. However, no matter how laboriously they searched their respective archives, the historians could not find mention of the restriction of flight to males, and some, to their credit, commented on the inclusive nature of the words "peasantry" and "populace," which they argued meant that everyone, regardless of race, gender, class or religious preference, had been given the power to fly.

VI

These studies went along with the curious observations in many of the documents that whenever a dispute ensued during flight, or an act of bigotry or racial or social intolerance occurred, the promulgator immediately lost altitude, as if he or she were being pulled back to earth. Continued indulgence in such behavior resulted in the loss of flying powers by the person or persons, or even townships, involved for however long the behavior lasted—a situation that in at least two instances, one recorded in Persia by the chronicler Abdul ibn Kassim, and the other by the Indian court poet, Gopal Chaudhuri, resulted in the subjects' suicides from despair at no longer being able to fly.

In most instances, a period of repentance, during which a readjustment of attitude took place, was enough to restore the transgressor's ability to fly, although the Belgian behaviorist Monica Somers sees no reason to doubt that chronic offenders suffered permanent suspension.

VII

Such examples make it clear that human flight was contingent on a capacity to tolerate extremes that was as much mental as it was physical. In other words, the physical ability to fly was at least partially dependent on finding an attitude of acceptance toward the ideas and opinions of others.

This postulate, first advanced by the Italian historian Luigi Gambini in 1968, was followed two years later by his encyclopedic study of various aspects of the flight phenomenon based on documents collected from around the world. The documents proved that the best of the flyers, "the athletes of the air," as he termed them, were those who had "neutralized their belligerent, envious, and dogmatic attitudes."

It was only a year later that Sven Angstrom, the Norwegian microbiologist, put forth the theory that the physical ability of flight was stimulated by a mental quietude which fostered the release, "in layman's terminology, of a 'flight' solution into the DNA component of the cell."

Although they were unaware of it at the time, Gambini and Angstrom had discovered not only the causes that enabled human flight to occur, but the very reasons which, in the end, destroyed it, as the Chilean naturalist, Francisco Podia, demonstrated in 1986. In his own words: "The coming of 'the athletes of the air,' as Gambini calls them, those perfectly adjusted beings who synchronized their physical and mental states into finely tuned instruments, so they could soar and swoop with acrobatic freedom, thereby enjoying the pure aesthetic pleasures of flight itself, was the undoing of the human ability to fly.

"As more and more people attempted to perfect themselves in this way, so their flying would lift them to the heights of enjoyment, they lost the balance that was necessary to maintain the phenomenon, for they abandoned contact with their earthly selves, neglecting the worldly concerns which sustain both body and mind. Specifically, their physical and mental toleration became so great, so laissez-faire, that it no longer existed, creating a chemical imbalance in the cell which caused the destruction of the flight capability. Add to this that 'the athletes of the air' were so intent on perfecting their flying techniques that they starved their bodies, and there is a strong possibility that in the process they shriveled the tissue-producing chemical which allowed the DNA molecule to manufacture the cell's oxygen-storing ability.

"At the same time as the young people, wearing colorful costumes of their own design so they could be identified from the ground, tumbled and somersaulted through the heavens, outraced eagles and clouds, and executed their movements with an almost angelic grace, more and more farmlands went unplanted, the towns and their economies fell into neglect, and the principles formulated by the town councils of the air and adopted by the populace fell into disuse and were forgotten, like the abandoned thatch-roofed cottages which dotted the countryside.

"As matters became economically chaotic in the towns and cities, the inhabitants began accusing one another of being the cause of the catastrophe, resorting to arguments based on religious, racial or social prejudices. Meanwhile, the children, oblivious to what was going on below, feverishly

fluttered and flapped high above in their gaily-colored costumes, not notic-
ing as their friends, one after another, stalled in mid-flight and, a moment
later, plummeted to the ground, although the next instant they too were
falling through the air, joining those bodies that were sprinkling the land-
scape like a shower of pebbles, until the sky was empty and windswept for
as far as the eye could see, and once more the world descended into bar-
barism."

The Words

When we sleep, the words inside us slide from their hiding places like thieves and assassins in a Renaissance city.

It is after midnight, but there are all these figures, muffled in cloaks or slipping from one pillar to another in black capes, who whisper and bicker, or come upon one another unexpectedly in the dark.

One stabs another in a shadowy arcade, and leaves the body where it falls. At the edge of a piazza, four ruffians, growling and cursing, carry off a drunken student in a burlap sack.

The facades of townhouses are still and dark, although whimpers and sighs and raspy snores flutter from the partially open windows, their meanings blurred by the fountains burbling in the squares.

The quiet everywhere is stippled by these sounds, as if the buildings were restless and muttering.

A shout. Lights flare at windows. Torches dot a piazza. It seems the body has been discovered.

But the sounds are confused, the reports garbled. Is it war, disease, the birth of an heir in the prince's palace?

A bell booms in a cathedral tower. The sound rushes in all directions over the tile rooftops.

A mile or two down the road leading to the city's west gate, a peasant in a cart lets his donkey guide him home as he sings of love, death and the joys of a simple life.

A Game of Chess

I have recently read that Hernando De Soto, captain in Charles V's expeditionary forces in The New World, taught the most high Inca chieftain Atahualpa to play chess during the chieftain's imprisonment in 1532, those uncertain months before the cutthroat Pizarro decided it would be best if Atahualpa were dead, because the body of a nation without its head.....

I looked up from the book and wondered whose life such information changes. Mine? Yours? No one's?—except, of course, Atahualpa's and, in a different way, Pizarro's and DeSoto's.

I had learned as a boy that De Soto discovered the Mississippi River in 1541 and died exploring it, his body in its armor heaved into the river, where it sank like a cannon ball, while his men, alone and terrified in the wilderness, wept.

In 1946 my uncle, who would fail in ten businesses and end his days as a gentle orderly in the Long Island Hospital for the Insane, drove a two-door forest-green sedan called a De Soto, and while sitting in the passenger seat next to him I'd stare for what seemed hours at the center of the steering wheel, where a medallion depicted the profile of the old conquistador with Spanish helmet and pointed beard. The medallion was colored gold and looked like a coin on a circular bed of crimson silk.

Years later, when I lived near the Mississippi, I remembered the shadowy interior of my uncle's car and his childlike laughter as he steered us north and south on our expeditions through the wilds of Brooklyn for a bottle of milk. His hands, displaying the only confidence he ever had, gripped the steering wheel where the medallion glowed like a saint's medal within the circle of his arms.

And when I walked along the Mississippi's banks, the brown water sliding by me, I would picture the muddy current like a drowned wind dragging through De Soto's upturned rib cage. Half sunk in the silt beside it, the rusted remains of arquebuses, swords, and armor every so often released a particle of rusted metal to the current as it sped southward, twisting and turning and tumbling the particle end over end with the bone flakes of Ojibwas and Dakotas, carrying them with uprooted tree trunks and bloated cows all the way to the Gulf of Mexico.

Now I follow those waters fanning out in the Gulf, cross Mexico and work my way south along the Andes to a side room in the stone fortress of Cajamarca where De Soto sits across a chessboard from Atahualpa. Hernando is holding up the knight on horseback with one hand and pointing to it with the other, and saying in exaggerated Spanish, "He arrives on horseback, prancing two steps to the side and one step forward. He never comes straight at you. So beware."

Which one is it then—Atahualpa reaching for the piece, or Hernando holding it from him—who a moment later laughs my uncle's childlike laugh?

Why My Signature Is Not on the Declaration of Independence

When my turn came to sign, I found there had been no place left for my signature. If Hancock hadn't taken up so much space at first with his ostentatious loops and slopes, Williams would have left me room, possibly. But when he bent low, squinting at the bottom of the page, and then scratched his quill against the parchment with a flourish, I knew, even before he signaled me with a shake of his head, that I needn't bother striding to the table. I returned to my chair in silent protest.

I'd known from the start that Hancock and the others did not want me to sign, although, as their token Jew, I was there solely for that purpose.

The entire assemblage, fifty or more and their friends, were jubilant. They had forgotten the sweltering heat and were congratulating one another, hurrahing and slapping backs—all wigs, waistcoats, grins and sweaty cheeks. Some, Adams in particular, were weeping. No one said anything about the absence of my signature. I sat alone in the middle of the merriment.

"What did I tell you," said a voice at my ear. It was Ranzini, who had been standing with the crowd in the back of the hall. As usual, his breath was rotten with garlic. I said nothing.

"When they removed the section condemning slavery, I knew there was no chance for you or me," he said.

So he'd been right, the fat Italian, with his grocery stores and Virgin births.

I was looking at Jefferson. He didn't seem to be disturbed by the changes in his original document, as, earlier in the day, I had overheard Franklin say he was. He stood with his usual aristocratic calm, accepting congratulations from all sides with a nod.

The striking of the slavery section hadn't bothered me, either. After all, you can go just so far.

The Kiss

Paris. July 7, 1792. The Revolution is about to collapse. For weeks the representatives, cursing and shouting, have scurried from group to group, or muttered behind each other's backs in the halls of the Assembly, unable to agree, it seems, on anything, as the food shortage continues and reports of invading armies, plots and counterplots, increase in number and wildness every hour.

Outside, crowds roam the streets, armed with pikes, pick-axes, and flint-locks spiked with fixed bayonets.

The representatives have taken to yelling and railing at one another at every session of the Assembly. They are doing so this morning as the abbé Antoine Adrien Lamourette rises from his seat. He raises his right arm for silence from his 700 colleagues, some of whom are dozing, others reading newspapers, while the majority whisper feverishly or declaim in small groups.

"*Liberté,*" he calls, and everyone turns to listen. "*Egalité, fraternité,*" he says. "*L'amour.*" Only love can save them, brotherly love. This is what the Revolution is all about and why they are there. They should pledge to hold that love as their first principle, he says, and seal the vow with a kiss.

For a moment no one moves. Then all at once the representatives, enemies and friends, are cheering, throwing hats in the air, embracing one another, kissing and laughing, as tears course down their faces.

It is only a gesture, of course. Within the hour, they will be bickering and arguing again, and within two months the Paris mob will supplant the debates with the rising of August 10th and the September Massacres.

To me, however, Lamourette and his proposal, and the Assembly's spontaneous reaction to it, is a reminder. When I'm most in despair at the hatreds and brutalities of my fellow humans, I think of him and his kiss, and I imagine that some kind of natural order, neither moral or religious, is at work in us—a twitch in our cells, a speck in our chromosomes—that tries to guide us back on course; and that even in the most tumultous human interactions it makes itself known.

Could the abbé's name really be a coincidence? Lamourette. In English it means "a little love."

Guillotine

Doorway without a door. We approach it with everyone pushing at our backs, shouting in our ears, shoving us forward, flies and mosquitoes buzzing around our heads. What nobility we have we leave behind.

The room on the other side looks like the one we're in—full of faces, buildings, clouds, traffic beyond the square—but we don't want to cross *that* threshold.

The advice "Don't look up" comes with a chuckle from the unshaven ruffian who breathes tobacco and onions in our faces, as if it is all a fraternity prank, the one with a bucket of water teetering on the lintel overhead.

We know what's waiting above: God's steel tooth ready to careen from the sky and bite off our heads.

Full length mirror without the glass. We cannot see ourselves, only cheering crowds who look like us, who cheer as we did. And that's the most frightening prospect of all, the world going on without us as if we've never been here, and we'll have to tell our secrets to the worms.

So we approach the doorway, twitching and trembling, and kneel before that other room, poking our heads through to the other side, as if praying or begging indulgence. But suddenly, unexpectedly, we picture ourselves as children on our knees, peeking into the maid's bedroom as she undresses.

That's the biggest joke of all, but we can't turn around to tell anyone. Will we never get serious? Probably not. Besides, our necks are resting so comfortably now in the wooden groove, which seems to have been hollowed especially for us, that we don't care if we go to our graves without giving one more instruction or bit of advice.

And so with faces looking down into a soiled basket like the ones old women carry to market, we take our leave with a final image that brings an idiot cackle to our departing lips—the picture of a head in the woven darkness, bumping among the other vegetables like a cabbage.

Teplitz, 1812

Coincidentally taking the waters in Teplitz at the same time, Goethe and Beethoven walked out of town arm in arm one afternoon. The cobbles, the soft sunlight, the road leading through the countryside to the Austro-Hungarian border, and ambling toward them the entire Imperial family out for a stroll—the Empress, Archduke Rudolph, courtiers, ladies-in-waiting, guards.

Goethe withdraws his arm, steps to the side, and bows so deeply his nose nearly touches the ground. Beethoven scowls, jams his three-cornered hat on his brows and saunters through the royal crowd, the Empress nodding to him and the Duke raising his hat. Goethe doesn't look up until the procession has passed.

I come back to this scene again and again: when the eighteenth century, and all those centuries before it, humbly make way for the past; when all the learned responses, customs, attitudes and values pulsing through Goethe—customs accumulated from Greek and Roman times and the barbarian invasions, customs merging with practices developed by medieval princes and Renaissance monarchs—make the poet bow.

Beethoven is the nineteenth century and the future, almost a naughty boy clomping through the royal ranks, gleeful at his impudence and new-found power. Royalty should make way for artists, dreamers, and captains of the future, his action seems to say.

After the procession passes, Beethoven berates the poet joyously.

Goethe will never forgive the composer, determining that "...he is an utterly untamed personality, not entirely in the wrong if he finds the world detestable, but he does not thereby make it more enjoyable for himself or for others."

Later, Beethoven writes of his behavior toward the royal family and of teasing his illustrious companion, "It was the greatest fun in the world!"

The Mussorgsky Question

The Mussorgsky question is an intriguing one: Should he be taken seriously as a composer, or was he merely a talented dilettante? Balakirev said, "His brains are weak." Tchaikovsky considered him to be talented but concluded that "he has a narrow stature and lacks the need for self-perfection." Tolstoy dismissed him by saying, "I like neither talented drunks nor drunken talents!"

A heavyset man with a clown's red nose and eyes that seemed circled by charcoal, Mussorgsky was drunk much of the time and at the end lived in a single room strewn with plates of half-eaten food and empty vodka bottles.

No one knew, however, that Mussorgsky was Dostoyevsky's greatest creation. So great, he sprang from the novelist's pen full-grown—and very drunk—on a stormy night in 1839, when Dostoyevsky, dreaming of becoming a writer, was an eighteen-year-old student at the school of Military Engineering.

Yet over the next forty-one years, the author didn't know where to place Mussorgsky: he was too talented to play Sonya's father or any of the other drunks who stumble through the pages of Dostoyevsky's novels.

Nevertheless, the author never abandoned the idea of using Mussorgsky, and put him on the Nevsky Prospekt until he found a suitable part for him in one of his books.

As drunks will, Mussorgsky wandered away, bewildered by all the lights and jingling horse-drawn sleighs. He vaguely remembered that he was a minor clerk in the Department of Forestry and a former officer in the Preobrajensky Guards, but he didn't know how he came to be standing on that boulevard. Since he was a drunk, however, he went in search of the first tavern he could find to solve his confusion.

Like all Dostoyevsky characters, Mussorgsky was an idea surrounded by flesh and clothes, so single-minded and uncompromising, as ideas are, that he could never adjust to life. He had given up his army career to compose and lived only for music. Elegant, witty, perfumed and slim, he grew corpulent and shabby and would disappear for months on end, surfacing more disheveled and delirious than he had been before.

Periodically realizing that Mussorgsky was not where he had left him, Dostoyevsky would hunt him down and bring him home, making him wait in a straight back chair in front of his desk, while he sought a place for him in the novel he was currently writing. This would go on for weeks, Mussorgsky all the while sitting upright, licking his lips and looking moist-eyed around the room for bottles.

Other than physically, Mussorgsky was half-formed in every way, even in music, where his harmonies and structure were so "rough" and "wrong" that they inspired Rimsky-Korsakov, Ravel and others to revise and rescore them in the forms we know them today, although how much of the music is theirs and how much is this bumbling phantom's, who may have existed only as an uncomfortable but thrilling thought in their conventional minds, we will never know.

Dostoyevsky never used Mussorgsky. Those other drunks, Marmeladov and Snegirov, were minor figures who functioned perfectly as victims, sufferers at the hands of others. But Mussorgsky—Mussorgsky was special: he had the soul of an artist, and this Dostoyevsky did not know how to handle. Possibly Mussorgsky was closer to Dostoyevsky's character than the novelist dared to understand.

With the creation of Illusha's alcoholic father in *The Brothers Karamazov*, Doystoyevsky stopped trying to find a niche in his books for the composer. He put Mussorgsky on the boulevard and, shoving him forward, he withdrew for the last time.

Mussorgsky was more bewildered than ever. How was a character supposed to behave who was created for a book that was never written? How was he to function? What was he to do? We can appreciate these questions, Dear Reader, since, one way or another, we ask them of ourselves almost every day.

In the end, Mussorgsky composed three operas and a handful of song cycles and tone poems. All are poorly written. No wonder many consider him a dabbler in music.

Composer or dilettante? Is that the Mussorgsky question? Or is it about the model who inspired others to be better then themselves by being so single-minded, so dedicated to his art that alcohol was the only other thing that had a place in his life? His commitment was so uncompromising that he could never be believable as a character in a novel, or for that matter as a human being.

The Brothers Karamazov was published in December, 1880. Dostoyevsky died of hemorrhaging lungs on January 28, 1881. Six weeks later, on March 16, Mussorgsky, enfeebled and suffering from delirium tremens for the previous two months, died of a stroke.

Both men are buried in the graveyard of the Alexander Nevsky Monastery.

The People of the Boat

I

Watching the shaggy shoreline separate into rocks and trees, we experienced a moment of questioning as well as foreboding: Had we been driven here by exile or loss—the remnants of a ragged army in defeat; or had we undertaken the journey like a choir whose singing was a splendor that drove the ships in clouds of glory to this other world—this world that, one way or the other, offered a promise we had to believe in?

While we swung axes and sledgehammers, felled birch trees and pine, while we lashed logs into walls, tarred roofs, and boiled tallow—these questions drove our days: why were we building, for what purpose—His glory or our own? And what, in the end, was the promise we expected to be fulfilled?

II

The same questions were asked by those in the ships that followed, when they saw the jagged outlines of the cities we had built, although, admittedly, for us these questions were rarely put into words. They were more a feeling—a foreboding.

And the forebodings grew, along with the ghosts of the animals and the painted people we had scrubbed from the land in the same way we scrubbed sweat from our bodies and noxious dreams from our minds—in the same way we had erased the old customs and former languages from our memories.

III

What had been promised? Had we sought freedom here, or had we been seduced by images of gold and goods, which make each of our cities look like a maze of marketplaces?

Had we sought escape in coming, remembering the armies at our back, or, as we told the young, had we chosen—faces forward in the salt wind—to seek a home where our ideas would take root in the landscape?

Or were both conceptions, in the end, really one and the same?

IV

Those who arrive now expect to see the cities on their horizons. Many have memorized the skylines and the famous buildings, and those who come with the old questions soon forget them in a tumult of forebodings.

Almost everyone thinks the cities were promised them, or they think nothing at all. The marketplace explains their days: the putting on equals the taking off, the spending is nearly as important as the getting, and the words "desiring" and "praying" are interchangeable in daily speech.

V

The populace bustles through the streets, jostling those people, wild-eyed and mumbling, who wander among them like shipwrecked sailors, lost and penniless, in a land whose ways they cannot comprehend.

Storms gather behind the buildings, cloudbanks that rumble like old forebodings. "It is weather, only weather," the people say. "It will vanish in a deluge of rain." But by this even the newcomers mean a new kind of rain, one that bites at the buildings and streets like teeth in the jaws of avenging ghosts.

The Storyteller

for Eduardo Galeano

In the town there was a storyteller, an old man who told outrageous stories about brooms that were girls in swinging skirts and giants who were snoring volcanoes.

Not only did he tell the stories, he was in them, dancing so lustily with the girls in their crinkly skirts that they knew they were beautiful, even if they weren't; and placing a pond like a cup of water near the volcano, so the sleeping giant wouldn't wake with a parched throat and smother the village below with his fiery breath.

The old man told stories about how bars of soap, when rubbed diligently between the hands, turned into fish and swam around the sink, and how napkins, when folded the proper way, flew around the dining room after every meal.

All his stories were impossible but never cruel, even when he told about spanking the cat because it ate the goldfish that was, in reality, his wife, who had died of the flu fifty years before, or slapping his nephew because the boy had swept out the fireplace without crossing himself, not knowing that the ashes were the remains of the dead and should always be treated with respect.

The children crowded around the old man on street corners after school, or in the shadowy arcade near the marketplace on weekends. Their parents never objected to the old man and his stories, no matter how impossible the stories were, nor did they tell the children they were wasting their time by listening to him.

After he finished telling a story, the old man would sit back and smile, and the children would press around him and whisper their fears and wishes into his ears. And the next week, or even the next day, those secrets would miraculously appear in one of the old man's tales.

The old man's stories were told and retold everywhere in the town. He told them for more than forty years, and the children grew and told them to their own children, and continued telling them after the old man died.

This happened in another country, and may not be true. It was told to me by a student whose name I have forgotten. He said he knew the old man when he was a boy, and had seen the soap swimming and the napkins flying, and could see them now. He said that the old man had begun telling the stories five years after his wife's death, and that he had never remarried, and never had children.

The student believed that by telling his stories the old man imagined he had made the town children his own. I disagree. More likely the old man considered the stories to be his children, and he was sending them out to play with the children of the town. In this way, he populated the town with his offspring, and with every change the stories underwent on other tongues, with every shift of tone and nuance, with every added detail, they became his children's children, dressed in the latest fashion maybe, but preserving an essential family resemblance beneath their clothes.

I envied the old man his stories as I envied the student and the others who had heard them and believed them enough to let them take on a life of their own. I knew that in time the stories could become more real than the town and its inhabitants, especially if the townspeople, like my student, traveled to different places in the world and told them to the people they met.

Because of what the student told me, a little of the old man and his town resides in me now, even though I have forgotten the student's name and never knew the old man's name or the name of the town. Again, the stories may not be true. The student was something of a smirker, as I remember, and could well have fabricated the old man, the tales, and the town itself to impress the ears of a willing teacher who saw less and less in the world to marvel at. If so, his cleverness undid him, for he created a place that exists, as all such places do, beyond the wind that will continue after he and I are gone—the wind that whips sunlight and shadows before it as it hurtles through abandoned villages and silent ruins.

The Manual for
Twentieth-Century Man
(and Woman)

Behind the Celestial Bakeshop

Behind the celestial bakeshop, in a factory hazy with flour dust, the women with rolled-up sleeves and aproned bellies still pound the dough on long wooden tables.

Their arms are rosy and ripe, their sweaty faces shine, their breasts bobble in their blouses, as the heels of their hands hammer the shapeless lumps into loaves.

Listen to the thumping and drumming, the irregular rhythm of hundreds of hands beating the dough into shape, in each case the final smack as much like slapping the first breath from a child as sending the unbaked bread on its way.

Every night they slide their long-handled paddles in and out of the big-mouthed oven, shoveling the flat smoky loaves into waiting baskets, and sprinkling them with galaxies and stars.

I love these celestial croupiers. Their give and take is a comfort beyond reason.

As I settle into sleep each night, I picture these women as I did when I was a boy. They are going about their final chore of whisking the sky clean with their brittle brooms. When I close my eyes, those brooms scratch at my memory, not reminding me of worlds that have gone, but of worlds to come, just like the branches that every morning scraped the darkness from my bedroom window.

The Girl Who Became
My Grandmother

Every night after the household was asleep, the girl who became my grandmother rode her stove through the forests of Lithuania.

She would return by dawn, her black hair gleaming with droplets of dew and her burlap sack filled with fog-webbed mushrooms and roots.

"It's true," my grandfather said. "At first I followed, but I could never keep up." He would hear the clanging and rusty squeakings fade into the trees and, with a sigh, he would go home.

He accepted the situation until the night she left in the kitchen, as if she were riding in a coach pulled by black horses of wind.

Grandfather followed in the rest of the house, standing in the doorway to the now-departed room, bellowing threats as if urging the house forward at greater speed.

He caught her outside Vilna, when she stopped to get her bearings, and the house slammed into the stalled kitchen, grandfather tumbling through the doorway and hitting his head on the leg of a table.

"And where do you think you're going this time, Lady?" he groaned from the floor, rubbing his right ear.

The girl smiled down at him and, kneeling by his side, stroked his hair, but didn't say anything.

That was the last time the girl who became my grandmother went on a nocturnal outing. Soon after, they left for America.

In Brooklyn, she rode from one day to the next in the house he had built around her, watching the changing scene beyond the kitchen window.

It was then she became my grandmother, white-haired and smiling, never saying much of anything, even when the old man shouted from the other rooms. Not that he ever needed anything. He just wanted to be sure she was still there.

The Key to the Air

"Look, I can open the air," my uncle said one day when I was nine and we were strolling to the corner candy store. "I have the key. See?" he said, holding a hand above his head, as we passed dented trash cans full of cinders and bottles and soggy brown bags. "See?" he said.

"Yes," I lied.

"This is the key to the air," he said. "Watch. I slip it in, turn it this way, and pull the daylight open, like this."

The other side of the pale blue sky was midnight black sparkling with stars and moons, like a plain blue cloak lined with black satin embroidered with golden symbols.

"See it?" he said.

"Yes," I lied again, hoping even then that lying was a way to make the impossible true.

My Father's Hobby

My father's hobby—don't laugh—was collecting sneezes. No stamps or coins for him. "The stuff of life," he said, "of life."

My mother and brothers shook their heads, his friends smirked, but he hurt no one, was an honest electrician, and everyone eventually shrugged it off as a harmless quirk. As his closest friend, Manny Borack, told my mom, "It could be worse."

Dad would mount the sneezes on glass slides he carried in his pockets everywhere he went. Some sneezes resembled flower petals, others seafoam, amoebas, insect wings, still others fan-shaped fingerless foetal hands, splatters of raindrops, or empty cocoons.

Next he stained the specimens magenta, turquoise, egg-yolk yellow, and placed them in the glass cases that stood in all the rooms.

Late at night when the family slept, he'd arrange handfuls of the slides on the light table in his study, and, switching off the lamp, he would peer down at them and smile.

One night, a small boy with bad dreams, I crept terrified through the darkened house to the study. He was bent over his collection, his face, surrounded by darkness, glowing in the table's light, as his lips murmured something again and again.

I slid my small hand into his and listened. He was rocking back and forth, bowing to the slides. "God bless you," he was saying, "God bless."

The Head

for Kim Wolterbeek

My Uncle Ernie found a head in his bowling ball case. It was nearly a perfect fit, a "mob job. Probably drugs," said the cop as he flipped over the pages of his pad and tucked it into his shirt pocket.

Every time he bowled after that, my uncle couldn't avoid the notion that he was poking his fingers into the victim's nostrils and mouth. It put him off his game, and more often than not the ball would roll into the gutter.

"That's where they all wind up," his friend Solly said with a grin, "in the gutter," and he went rat-a-tat-tat with an imaginary machine gun.

My uncle didn't think that was funny, that and the other jokes about the Headless Horseman or how good it was that he was finally "getting ahead in the world."

"For chrissake! For chrissake!" he'd say, and "Let a guy have some peace. They don't even know who he is, for chrissake." But I couldn't understand if the guy he referred to was the victim or himself.

"Victim? What do they mean by that? He was someone. He coulda had a wife, maybe kids," my uncle said that Sunday at the family dinner.

"Take it easy," my father said, nodding to the other end of the table, where my grandmother sat. "Mama: remember?" But the old lady was patting my sister's hair and smiling, and hadn't heard.

Uncle Ernie looked at her, then leaned close to my father. "I mean, who was the guy, and how did his head get in my case?" he said in a scratchy whisper.

My father shrugged. He was the oldest of three brothers and the others were always asking him questions, which he inevitably answered with a shrug. "Coulda been anyone," he said. "You still keep the case in your locker at work?"

Uncle Ernie nodded.

"Coulda been anyone," my father said again. "You can't think about it no more. Forget it."

But Uncle Ernie couldn't forget it. After school I'd meet him when he got off work at the post office, and he'd drive me home. "They don't understand," he'd say, leaning toward me from the steering wheel. "Everyone else has a locker. Why mine? See what I mean? There's more to this than your dad thinks."

The kids at school knew about the head from their parents, and crowded around, asking if I'd seen it and what Uncle Ernie had said about it. That was the year Mr. Goodman told the class about head-hunters in the Amazon, how they shrank the heads and sewed the lips together and stitched the eyelids shut.

Shortly afterwards I began dreaming about the head. A hand was holding it by the hair in front of my face. The sewn lips were struggling against the threads, wanting to say something, and the eyelids fluttered and flew off like two moths, leaving the eyeballs bloodshot and swollen, staring into my eyes, as if the head was beseeching me to explain why it was unable to speak.

In two or three months the jokes and questions stopped, and my uncle's bowling game improved. It was about that time he met Aunt Sue, to whom, my father said with a smirk, he lost his head. After they married and had kids, Uncle Ernie would answer any questions, even questions about the head, with a shrug.

Eventually the head came to mean all the unanswered questions everyone had asked about it, even when the cop arrived at the house several months later and told Uncle Ernie and my father who the head belonged to. They shrugged. But I was too young to shrug. Besides, I had this weird idea that if I shrugged my head would fall off.

The Great Tree Scare

One day all the trees wiggled their toes.

"Whoa! Whoa!" some people said, crouching and holding their arms out for balance.

"Steady, boy. Steady," said others and patted the grass, thinking it was an earthquake.

No one was hurt, but, as many people said in their different tongues, "If you can't depend on the trees standing still, what can you depend on?"

That night as the planet entered the different zones of darkness, a blaring noise, full of metallic vibrations and guttural rumblings, rolled toward the earth from the sky, and a shimmering sound broke like the sea over forests, mountain ranges and meadows. For several minutes, the trees thrashed their arms in response.

Again, no one was hurt. Only acorns and pine cones, and on remote islands bombardments of coconuts, showered the ground. But people were alarmed. What would happen at dawn, or the next night?

Firemen and ambulance workers were ordered to stand by, armies and navies put on alert. Presidents and premiers sent special envoys to negotiate with the trees, but the diplomats couldn't find any trees willing to talk, and it soon became apparent that nothing could be done to control whatever might happen.

So the world waited. One day. Then two. At dusk on the fourth night after they had first moved, the trees released a sigh of such earthy spiciness that everyone on the planet gagged and coughed, engulfed for the moment by a cidery haze.

It was an exhalation full of apples and cherries, coconuts and figs, full of the scent of wet fur and the underside of stones, of mint and oranges and buried things, and those moist hidden places that are the origins of sweetwater limestone springs.

All these fragrances streamed from the trees, and in one aromatic heave, as if swept off the planet by a gigantic perfumed wing, they wafted fumes of earthly incense throughout the universe.

The next day, children everywhere built shrines of twigs and leaves under the trees, shrines which soon after parents replaced with carved boulders of almost animal grace, where sheltered candles were always kept lit. "These boulders are memorials," the politicians proclaimed, "which will commemorate our debt to the trees until the end of time."

Everyone, it seeemed, understood that the trees had not rebelled but had averted a catastrophe almost too big to be comprehended, while reminding us of something we should never have forgotten.

As for the trees, from the moment of their exhalation, my grandfather said, they have not stirred. This is a story he told me when I was a boy, and said that his grandfather had told to him. "To this day," he would say as we ambled through the park, "the trees move only their branches. Look, look there. Whenever you see the trees swaying their branches that way, they're waving a greeting to the heavens. See? It's like they're reassuring sun, moon and stars that everything's all right down here."

The Seduction of the Trees

Each night the trees imitate the birds they see flying during the day. They choose the darkness so they won't be seen flapping and flouncing like elephants with the souls of ballerinas.

It's so damn sad when you want to be something other than what you are, especially trees who get to stand outdoors in all sorts of weather and never catch even a sniffle.

And isn't it a ballerina's most secret wish to stand on one leg day after day without tiring, while birds flutter and nest in showers of song on her shoulders?

All this is the wind's doing. Every hour it returns to woo the trees, who refuse again and again but like you and me want to believe and are easily influenced.

The Drugstore

I remember when I was a boy passing the darkened drugstore at night, my footsteps following too close behind me, and how I would run when I saw the patina of bluish light radiating from the pharmacy in the rear of the shop.

I knew the light was left on to discourage thieves. But there was always a suspicion that Mr. Gold, the owner, a small man, round and bald, who smiled too blandly and never looked us in the eye, was working there alone on something forbidden.

Silhouetted against the light, shadows flailed and swooped, and I was sure he was cutting or pounding plants that squirmed and snatched at his hands, or draining a yellowish ooze from the rocks he had gathered in the park, as if he had lanced an abscess hidden in a seam of stone.

I was positive he would bottle that bubbling mess, and store that bottle, along with others, next to the cartons of pills he kept in the storeroom in back, cartons which shifted like bins of baby teeth in the dark.

Everyone in the neighborhood was certain that something unholy was going on. Why else would he remain in the store so late each night? "To do the books," he murmured and smiled when asked one morning by Mrs. Marks. "And to fill the orders for the following day."

I see him now in the bluish light, among ledgers and thumb-worn index cards, and no longer think those books were unholy texts, but lists of prescriptions and payment stubs, credits and debts he would check and double check.

Like all kids, I imagined ledgers and books whose pages fluttered like wings, and him holding them down with rocks from the park, so they wouldn't flap while he read, or fly around the room, blundering against boxes and jars. I imagined he could revive the dead, make flowers dance and shriek, and hold the pulse of time in the palm of his hand.

"Bills and medicine," he said with a smile, and shrugged, avoiding our eyes as he spoke.

I guess all of us back then, young and old alike, needed to believe it was something else, something that had nothing to do with tidy city parks, but with meadows and hillsides beyond the ocean's wintry waves, where forests were shrinking to shadows in landscapes most of us would never see and fewer and fewer of us remembered.

Calendar

I woke to cold sunlight on the window, and the squabbling of distant crowds. I followed the sound downstairs to the calendar tacked to the kitchen wall. The days of the month, small blank rectangles arranged in rows, were, I saw, windows in an apartment house, and leaning on the sills were the famous dead, presidents and poets, generals and revolutionists. Some were silently staring out at the kitchen's fragrant light, others were giving speeches, shaking their fists or yelling at the windows above and below them.

There were other, smaller sounds coming from the calendar, some almost indistinct, and I understood that each month was an apartment house waiting on its own street, with its own names at the windows, and that all twelve buildings were the principal edifices in the city of the dead.

And what of the nameless ones, I thought, those who had been neither poets nor generals, but had struggled to exist from day to day, raising families, dying from pneumonia or heartache—those who over the eons had drowned by the millions in floods or tidal waves, been buried by earthquakes, butchered by armies, and ordered obliterated by the visionary and the greedy; those nameless citizens who believed in a second coming, where sunlight would be as thick and sweet as honey, because one had to believe in something, or why endure it all?

Instinctively I knew that those nameless dead were muttering behind the ones at the windows, as unassumingly sharing the apartments with their famous counterparts as they had anonymously shared their times with them when they were alive.

Now every morning when I cross off another day from the calendar, I imagine I am closing a window on the voices in that apartment for another year. But just before I place an X over the window, I pause with pen raised, and bow my head, as if listening to directions from someone I have stopped on the street.

In the Attic Closet

In the attic closet, the moth, settled like a medal on grandpa's double-breasted business suit, hums and flutters as it munches. Grandma's brown fox wriggles and pants on the hanger.

On the floor beneath their hems, the overturned ashtray from Ocean Beach, Maryland, still sprinkles the air with the shrieks of teenagers above the wave roar, and the clumps of dust continue to lisp their only monologue to the floorboards, who never listen.

The floorboards are dreaming, as they always do, of standing in sunlight, sliding arms from their sides and lifting many hands toward the sky.

But when the dust clumps, still murmuring, lay their cheeks against the floorboards' chests, the floorboards don't shoo them away; they incorporate them into their dream, where they wrap their arms around them.

Angel Incident

An angel appeared in my study not too long ago: bedraggled, mussed hair, muttering to himself. Both wings lifted like ocean swells with every breath he drew or word he spoke. They seemed to have a life of their own; I couldn't take my eyes off them.

The angel kept muttering to himself. He was studying a crumpled, poorly folded map, the kind bought at gas stations: he opened panels and refolded them, peering repeatedly at the network of lines inside.

He knew I was there. Several times he looked up and smiled weakly—I nodded in reply—but he never asked me directions before he strolled through the wall near the window and was gone.

Of course, I never asked him if he needed help. It never occurred to me. At the time, I thought it was enough that we were in the same room together. I was wrong. We both were.

Smoking Cigars

When I smoke a cigar, I'm part of the earth again, but a wilder earth than municipal parks and public gardens. The wrapped brown leaves, brittle as autumn, smell like rotting fish and crumbling stone.

Even in an apartment high above the city, I become an element of the earth once more, when the cigar smoke enfolds me like the air inside a tomb.

I sit at a table opposite an empty chair when I smoke, and imagine the cigar is an earthen whistle through which I summon whatever ghost will come. Most of the time it's a leathery man, his skin as brown and thin as tobacco leaves.

We sit face to face across the table, not speaking, smoking the same cigar from opposite directions, my mouth clasping the unlit end, and his the fiery cinder whose glow must resemble the burning coal that sprang from the darkness to start the world.

He blows into the cigar as if blowing on the coal, and I suck until I am filled with the life beyond this one. When I exhale, he sips my living air through the pink nipple that scorches his tongue.

In church on Sundays, some people eat and drink the body and blood of their god. I consort with those who are less sublime, the ones who built the pyramids and tombs with their hands, and who vanished without hope of being revered or even remembered.

I Knew Better

Trumpeting loudly, an elephant charged out of a map of Africa in a book I was reading. There were others charging behind him.

All that saved me was the **n** after the **a** in an, our only protection from the fury of vowels, the fury that lies in wait for us in an eagle's talons or an orangutan's grasp.

I've known this since third grade—the dangers a book contains, and how we have to be careful the way we write or else an **o** in the ozone layer could widen into a lake, exposing us all.

"Mind your **p**s and **q**s," Mrs. Flannagan told us, and I do. It's a responsibility we all have.

As for the elephant, he stopped behind the **n**, as if on the other side of a boulder, and browsed unconcernedly, snuffling his trunk along the white ground. The others shuffled behind him, nuzzling one another with such tenderness that I wanted to reach around the rock and touch their warm sides. I didn't, of course. I knew better.

What Has to Be Done

All night the loose shutter bangs against the house.

"It's someone wanting to come in out of the rain," thinks the man seated at the table in the kitchen's yellow light.

"It's a wing beating to take flight," thinks the woman lying in the darkened bedroom.

The man knows he will not allow the dripping shutter to sleep in the hall, and the woman understands that if the wing succeeds in lifting the house, the house will veer in a circle after several feet and land with a plaster-cracking crash back where it sits now.

In the other bedroom, a child in a raincoat prepares to open the window and carry the cookies and milk he has saved to the damaged shutter. Then he will loosen a shutter on the other side of the house, so the house can fly away. He doesn't know where the house will go; he doesn't care. He just knows what has to be done.

The Story That Had Never Been Written

I first came across "The Story That Had Never Been Written" on one of those nights when the household was asleep and I was sitting up late reading. At such times a lonely protectiveness for those dreaming in the rooms around me evokes a melancholy close to anguish, which I'm sure has something to do with an enlarged sense of time passing created by the surrounding stillness.

Thumbing through a short story anthology I had just bought, I came across a title in the table of contents which interested me. However, when I turned to the page on which the story was supposed to begin, it wasn't there. I flipped the pages back and forth but still couldn't find it, and mildly annoyed I shut the book and went to bed.

The title in question was "The Story That Had Never Been Written," and during the next several months I found it listed in a half dozen other anthologies, but in each instance I could not locate the story on the page it was supposed to appear, or anywhere else in the book.

I could understand such an error happening in one volume, but the coincidence of it occurring in several was unthinkable: the omission had to be intentional.

A story without characters, without beginning, middle and end? A story that didn't exist? What did it mean? What could have drawn the editors to it? Indeed, *how* could the editors have been drawn to it?

My annoyance turned to curiosity, and finally I was intrigued.

I went to the town library and looked up the writer in a biographical dictionary, finding him mentioned in a short paragraph along with a bibliography of his books, which included three novels and a collection of stories.

His name was Elaard van Steen. He was born and had lived in a small Dutch town in the second half of the nineteenth century, where he had worked as a night brakeman at a railroad crossing outside of town. He had written his stories to while away the long nocturnal intervals between train passings, had never married, and died of leukemia six months short of his fortieth year. One of his novels, *Anguish*, had attracted some attention and had been translated into French and German, but critics of his own day thought that he had not come into his full powers by the time of his death. Recently, the article concluded, his short stories had received renewed interest and he was thought by some to be a precursor of the literature that explores the "psychological condition of modern man."

I checked out the book of short stories, noting that I was surprisingly sweaty as I did so. I refused to open the book before I got home, and then only when my wife and two sons had gone to bed. As I turned the first page, I smiled on once more noticing that I was perspiring and my fingers trembling.

I read the book through without looking at the table of contents. Except for several stylistic felicities and ironic reversals, the tales were almost to a narrative unexceptional. They concerned what one would have expected from a brakeman sitting alone with nothing to do for hours on end, as he put it "under the constant flowering of the botanical night."

There was a story about an Arab sitting by a fire under desert stars; a Dutch rubber plantation owner in the East Indies whose wife leaves him; a young girl suffering from insomnia because when she did sleep she always dreamed of falling while on her ice skates, floundering about, with everyone around her refusing to help her up. Stories of frustrated wives, lonely children, stifled men.

I sighed and turned to the table of contents, and there to my surprise—although I can't say why—was the title of the story which had drawn me to the book in the first place. "The Story That Had Never Been Written" was listed as the twelfth of the fifteen stories, but I couldn't remember what it was about. I flipped to the indicated page and once again found nothing—or more accurately, I found what I had in the other collections, the next story listed.

The story I was looking for simply did not exist. It never had. I slammed the book shut and sat there with the sound receding in all directions through the quiet house.

My wife called dreamily to me from several rooms away, but I didn't answer. What could van Steen have been thinking of?

I pushed myself out of the chair, almost claustrophobic with annoyance, and sauntered through the house, out the back door and into the shadowy yard.

The sky bloomed around me. I felt infinitesimally small beneath it, and I thought of van Steen seated night after night under this same sky, contemplating his aloneness and his early death.

And all at once I knew the meaning of "The Story That Had Never Been Written." It was a sign for the blankness, the emptiness of all those stories van Steen knew he would never write, maybe of all those stories that had never been written, or would never be told, by anyone else.

But van Steen had been mistaken. Viewing himself under a nineteenth-century sky, he imagined that he had one of two choices. It never occurred to him that each choice contained not only its opposite but every other choice as well. And as I reflected on this I thought I could hear the people turning over in their beds in the houses around me. I thought I could hear them murmuring and calling out, and I was calling back that everything was all right, don't worry, I'm here, as time grew large around me and passed me by in the stillness of the story that is always being written.

Who Can Tell the Dreamer
From the Dream?

Do we dream the landscape, or does the landscape dream us, as we scurry over it appraising the views, fencing acres, and building the house we always dreamed of?

Even the house, shifting late at night, may be aware of its occupants as we are aware of the dreams and desires inside us, the rooms like compartments for different wishes where we sit, sleep, and eat, performing what the house wants us to perform, which is what the landscape dreams the house will do.

The landscape, with the oceans and continents, rivers and pastures curving over it, may be a ball that rolls into the corner of a dark field where no one can find it, and its houses and people may be glittering splotches of microbes stuck to its surface as it rolls.

Several hours ago, the boy who threw the ball went home to the farmhouse a mile down the road, where he was scolded at supper for losing the ball, while his sister, a year older than he, smirked and stuck out her tongue, a slight which the boy, now asleep in his room, will not forget.

We can no longer see the ball or the field, but several windows of the farmhouse are bursting with light, along with the windows of a dozen other houses down the road. Beyond them, the light-cluster of a suburb sparkles in the night but is almost obliterated by the melding of a million light sources from a city in the distance.

All this—the ball, the field, the farmhouses, the suburb, and the city ablaze with light—is a scene in a paperweight that sits on a desk in an old man's study. When he gets bored or is deep in thought, he idly raises the paperweight and shakes it, watching the snow fall on the scene inside and remembering a trip he went on with his parents. It was on that trip that his father bought him the paperweight as a souvenir—that same father who one night not long after went out for cigarettes and never returned.

For a long while after his father's disappearance, the old man's mother had grieved, moaning and clutching her chest, several times attempting to smash the paperweight, which each time the old man managed to wrestle from her grasp.

Eventually the mother met a car salesman, and one night when she was drunk she told her son that she had never been happier, that his father had not been much in bed.

The old man had never forgiven his mother for this and had begun having doubts about himself, doubts that were conveyed by tremors of anxiety which, when he absently lifts the paperweight, are felt inside from the city to the suburb, from the farmhouses to the field, all the way to those rivers and pastures stuck to that spot on the rolling ball where the house shifts around us in the middle of the night.

Explanations of Night

Was it as my grandfather said, that hearing boots crunch in the intergalactic snow outside his hut, our Grandfather of grandfathers blew out the candle near the open window, sending splashes and specks of wax into the darkness, where they instantly froze?

Or was it as my grandmother insisted, that tears were caught in the black folds of a widow's shawl?

So much fear and so much sorrow. Is that what they saw, looking up at the stars each night?

Powered by a buzzing pile of metal across town, five lamps light this room, connected to the pile by wires as sensitive as nerves. The rest of the house is dark, as dark as it is outside, where only the streetlamps, connected to the same wires, provide light for watchmen and whatever wanderers are abroad tonight.

All these patterns of light are patches of illumination on the darkened continent, where the headlights of cars creep along invisible roads, going somewhere, sure of their destinations, so sure.

Waitresses

Late at night, lonely men—truckdrivers, unshaven hitchhikers to anywhere, or college boys half-drunk on being eighteen—watch them approach with their bouffant hairdos and swinging hips, and imagine pumping into them on beds like slowly revolving carousels.

These are the women who wait with pad and pencil to take down anything the men want. The young ones leave their top buttons undone, know the whole room loves them, and write the orders like billets-doux. The older ones, when business is slow, sit at the counter, tap their cigarettes in plastic ashtrays, and stare at the darkness beyond the window panes.

The banter that goes back and forth between these women and the seated men is a half-remembered ritual that mimics the prescribed dialogues that took place in Hindu and Egyptian temples thousands of years ago, when diaphanously gowned priestesses of Annapurna or Isis, rubies and emeralds glittering in their hair, received the pleas of dusty, wild-eyed supplicants, and later when delicate damsels, in a dream of castles, listened to the scorching passions of delirious young men.

In Oregon or Kansas, wind and rain buffeting the plate glass windows, the men ask for fried eggs and coffee, orange juice, bacon and potatoes, meaning something else, something they've forgotten how to put into words but hope the waitresses are writing down, trusting that these women understand what they really want to say.

When the waitresses saunter from the table with their requests, the men follow them with their eyes to the chamber of fires, where cymbals clang and holy oils smoke, where birds' eggs are broken and cooked, meats from sacrificial animals prepared, and the tropical elixirs and steaming potions brewed that will send these pilgrims into the night once more, ready to travel separate roads in search of holy places, the image of these women at roadside stops shining in their heads like the holy medallions swinging from their rearview mirrors.

Kisses

When I was a boy, the kiss waited in the hall or around the corner, always outside the classroom where our voices droned.

When I was awake it hovered in my dreams, and when I slept it fluttered beside my bed, holding its breath.

I could tell you that the kiss was like a butterfly, but you've probably already thought of that.

Of course, there was more than one, there was a skyful of kisses migrating toward me from another hemisphere, but they hadn't arrived, not yet. They were just over the horizon, although their perfume billowed ahead, engulfing me in clouds of cidery scents that watered my eyes and tugged away my breath.

Each spring the kisses hid behind bushes and trees, but even though I dashed from trunk to trunk, even heard the beating of their wings, I could never find them.

Then all at once they appeared, swarming over me until I couldn't breathe—not butterflies, but a yapping kennel of kisses, all on show, and I was the judge. There was the woman walking her poodle kiss, snout in the air; another with her bulldog growling in my face; and a third with her nibbling Pekingese.

Then came the lion-licking kisses, the bear-nuzzling, pig-rooting, horse-teeth kisses;

kisses like sharks and barracuda sliding around a drowning man and bumping against him, or piranha kisses that shot straight at me, clicking their spiky teeth.

There were deep-throated lily kisses, open-mouthed orchid and daffodil kisses;

rainstorms of kisses, blizzards of kisses, hurricanes, typhoons, even tornados of kisses.

Kisses, kisses—kisses finally cold and far away.

In the end it was windswept planet kisses, sun-spurt kisses, showers of static, cosmic belches and glittering galaxy kisses, kisses like star systems erupting as soundlessly as exploding hearts, icy black silence kisses, and faint, almost imperceptible radio-signal kisses that twitter even now from deep in the night and wake our children and grandchildren with a start.

When God said, "Let there be light, " his lips kissed each other, some people say, and the spark from that contact flared through the dark and was the first day.

The Evil Eye

My friend Larry Fixel, a writer attuned to the subtle shifts and peccadillos of the mind, remarks that two European poets of his acquaintance, both formidable intellectuals and surrealists, believe in the evil eye. As he says this, he nods his head meaningfully, as if I were to understand that even today vestiges of medievalism survive.

But I'm not surprised. The surrealists, in their quest to catch notions of the subconscious the instant they take wing, are the descendants of the alchemists who wanted to capture the soul's breath and separate it from the body, or, in cruder terms, change lead into gold.

Their lineage includes shamans and magicians as well as scientists—no wonder they believe in evil and supernatural events.

They sit all night by the mountain of the psyche, as their forebears did, waiting in the blue pre-dawn light for the moment a shower of yellow butterflies, as elusive as sunbeams, scatters from deep inside the mountain.

Larry is already at work in a stream nearby, patiently panning in the chilly water, and I am seated on a rock examining a handful of gravel.

The stream wriggles through a meadow and a forest, lisps by a hillside strewn with several farmhouses and dotted with hundreds of dozing sheep, and slips unobtrusively into the sea.

Could the sun that rises over such a scene be a devil's burning eye? Medieval monks thought the sun was God's eye overseeing the landscapes he had made, and for years I've thought a blind but holy eye looks down on us each day.

Who's to say? I have another friend, a sculptor dying of cancer, who thinks that whether we're asleep or sitting with clenched fists behind the window shades, the sun rises over us like a furnace every morning and gilds the planet like a golden pendant with its light.

Swallows

I've seen them at sunrise and sunset in Greece, Italy, and California, dipping and swooping over the fields; skyfuls of them streaking this way and that, snatching up insects in mid-flight, but looking as if they were searching the earth for something lost or forgotten.

From a distance, a dozen or more resemble bits of paper thrown at the horizon. But they are never scattered by the wind: they slice through it, flitting over the stubble wherever they want.

Wings arched like medieval bows, heads like arrows about to be launched, they wait on the frescos of Minoan palaces or on the enclosed walls of Egyptian tombs, buried for thousands of years in stone-stunned darkness, ready to take wing the instant a thief or scientist's torch flares into their night.

Keats and the others can have their nightingale. I'll take the swallows skittering from crumbling walls or bursting from tombs and twittering over fields everywhere on the planet: they are so much like words urgently wanting to be written, almost insisting they be chosen, as they snap up nuances almost too tiny to be seen, and seek their places on an empty page.

The Letter

I found the letter in a book I bought at an outdoor theatre turned flea market every weekend. It was June 1995 in a small town on the California coast.

The book was Tolstoy, *Anna Karenina*, and the letter was tucked between pages 434 and 435, where a delirious Levin, the day after he's proposed to Kitty, visits her parents' home. The letter—pinkish, sealed, not mailed, faintly redolent of talcum, like a pressed flower—was from a Sarah Harris, dated inside October, 1939.

Yes, I opened it and read how fine the trip was from Des Moines back to Cincinnati, suspecting nuances and unworded passages I had no way of understanding—or, more accurately, deciphering—to go along with what I took to be the mute appeal to Carl Bigelow, 913 McKinley Avenue, Des Moines, Iowa, in the final paragraph: "There didn't seem time for me to say all the things I needed to. Do you feel the same?"

The Tolstoy was a book club's bonus edition bound in grey leatherette. Had Sarah Harris purposely placed the letter between those pages depicting Levin and Kitty's jubilant betrothal? I had no way of knowing, and refused to suppose. However, I resealed the letter, affixed fresh stamps to the envelope, and sent it on.

The Woman Who Didn't Live Right

There was a woman who didn't live right. She lived left. Everything she experienced was reversed, as in a mirror.

"I hate you," she told her boyfriend, meaning the opposite, and she always turned her car in the wrong direction on one-way streets.

Admirers said she was totally right-brained, and marveled at her commitment to revolutionary creativity; but those closest to her, especially her four husbands and her children, found her impossible to live with.

She never arrived at appointments on time. In fact, she never arrived at appointments at all. And after announcing plans to travel to Europe by boat, she went to Australia by plane.

When she murmured in post-orgasmic serenity, "I want to have your child," she meant, of course, that she definitely didn't want to have it, and the proposed babe wandered through a bardo existence for which Tibetan Buddhists could find no precedent in any of their texts.

This babe, in fact, was found frowning and gnashing its teeth, a hissing demon, on a mountain road in Peru by holy men searching for the next Dalai Lama. The demon child, they reported, had entered the world through a tear in the universe and had ushered in an army of other howling and hissing creatures of its acquaintance who it dispatched to every continent, and all of this the holy men attributed to the woman who didn't live right.

Almost simultaneously, of course, the holy men excused the woman, saying the demon invasion was meant to happen and was the next stage in the world's development.

When informed of all this, the woman said she felt neither guilt nor remorse, which meant she felt both.

It still would have been too late for us all if the woman hadn't realized that the life she had left had to be put right. That was the bridge she had to cross from the life she had led to the one we all lead trying somehow to get to the next day.

"Hello," she said to the first person she encountered after crossing that bridge, and to her own and everyone else's astonishment, she no longer meant "good-bye."

Not that this sent the demon children wandering once more through Bardoland, or turned them into dust, or into so much non-thought. Nor did it allow us to live happily there or after.

But, as the Tibetans observed and we and now she can agree, it meant that it definitely wasn't the end, just another in a series of endless beginnings.

The Man Who Kicked the Universe in the Ass

There was a man who kicked the universe in the ass. It was grazing in his backyard. The universe had grazed in the backyard before, pressing its behind against the house from horizon to horizon, morning, noon and night. But the man hadn't noticed it until that day.

"Get off my property, you," the man shouted, and swung his leg, shoetip sailing with pinpoint accuracy at what looked like an elephant's behind. It was larger, of course, the same color gray, but not wrinkled, rather a cloud-like substance through which the man's shoe sank, so upsetting his balance he almost fell.

"Now I've done it," the man thought. All his life he had been a grouch and complainer, finding fault with the way his neighbors kept their lawns, and the way his wife drove the car, overcooked the eggs, and burnt the toast. He knew that one day he'd go too far, but when he woke that morning he hadn't known that day had come. "Now I've done it," he murmured, waiting for the universe to look around and exhale streams of flame from its nostrils, or belch axe-edged galaxies at his property and him.

The universe, however, takes a long time to look around. That morning its head was sunk in a bush of flowering stars in the garden beyond the man's imagination, and it couldn't be bothered, or it couldn't distinguish among all the sensations bombarding it, to identify that one.

So nothing happened, and after a few minutes the man relaxed and went into the house, muttering, "and good riddance to you," choosing not to notice that the universe was still in the backyard, and hadn't even budged. Soon the man was grumbling again, this time about how the universe, like everything else, paid no attention to him.

It had, of course. Somewhere it registered that tiny kick, just as the man's wife was aware, as she slept two nights later, of the mosquito lancing into the hillside of her left buttock. Although she didn't wake, that twinge entered the swirling dreams she tried to explain to the man each day, dreams of gardens with jewellike flowers on which she continually fed.

How I Came to Own the World

We enter the world with nothing and leave it the same way. In between, we pile up appliances, canned foods, automobiles, bank accounts, real estate —hills of goods we stand in front of, as if posing for a photograph that shows our worth.

I owned nothing because I wanted nothing, one of the destitute in spirit as well as material wealth, until a curious thing happened: I read in the newspaper about a man who had murdered several people. The paper referred to the dead as "the murderer's victims," as if in some way he owned them.

The phrase excited me, but I had no desire to kill, rob or maim. Still, the excitement was there, and soon I was intrigued by the idea that I could plan a murder or robbery, go through all the motions, but not commit the act.

I managed to get the floor plans of several mansions and banks, in my spare time followed unsuspecting women for months on end. I owned them. I owned everyone to whom I turned my attention, since I permitted them to keep what they had, including their lives. I stood in front of store windows, admiring the furs, paintings, television sets, thinking, "They're mine, all mine. All I have to do..."

Everyone was indebted to me, as if to a banker, for allowing them to keep their necklaces, stereos, cars. These things are theirs on loan. I finance them, so to speak.

Now I walk the streets of my neighborhood, town or city, proud of my apartment buildings, parks and museums. I nod to all the passersby with a benevolence I never imagined existed. Each tilt of my head or tip of my hat signals, "Think nothing of it...You're welcome... Happy to do it."

I've never felt so good about myself. Of course, there are problems, decisions to be made, certain moral conundrums involving how I should allow lands and people to be treated and who should be permitted to do what to whom. But I don't want to bore you. I just wanted to let you know how I came to own the world. Run along. We'll speak again after you've had a chance to look around. Have you tried my restaurant on the corner?

Beware of Men Who Part Their Hair

Beware of men who part their hair, who every morning stand before the mirror and uncover a path though the underbrush. They are opening roads for all sorts of commerce.

A friend imagined he was making a highway for his thoughts. When he put the comb back on the sink, he could hear the engines over the horizon. Soon the highway was crowded not only with last year's pickups and station wagons, but with models of his own invention. Car designers would take him to lunch just to stare at his head, or sneak into his bedroom at night to study the vehicles that might come down the road while he slept. Poor guy. He threw himself under the wheels of a moving van bringing an attic full of memories that he didn't want to remember.

Hitler parted his hair and, among other things, invented the autobahn.

The Inca highways zigzagged over the tops of the highest mountains. They're still there, windswept, a trail for howling ghosts, a roadway of memories we can no longer remember, even if we wanted to, because Pizzaro parted his hair down the middle.

Gardeners are among the worst. They part the land's hair, always weeding, pulling up bushes by the roots, laying out everything in orderly rows like botanists with the souls of accountants who build bonfires of the earth's assets, bonfires that resemble bookburnings and *autos-da-fé* where saints and heretics alike breathe their last in the billows of the earth's smoke.

And look at the trails in the jungle. As we uncover them, they are no longer trails, but bald spots on the planet's head. Each tree is a hair falling. When it hits the ground, the silence erupts like thunder and reverberates for miles. The Indians run in circles and cover their ears with their hands, but the blood drips between their fingers, and their straw villages, exposed for the first time to the sun's glare, are overturned and put to the match, the women carried away screaming by men in pants and shirts with parts in their hair.

Although we can't see them, Indian runners, carrying memorized messages, lope from one smoldering village to another. They quickly learned it was best to stay under the trees that are left. Spears and bows in the hands at their sides, they jog through the shadows, with painted faces, avoiding clearings, their footfalls like leaves kissing the earth. "After they've passed," the man at the cantina, with pale hands and a part in his hair, told me, "you don't even know they were here."

All the Animals Are Gone Now

All the animals are gone now, except the cats.

First the insects vanished from every village, town, and city square. Then came reports of elephants and zebras erased from sun-rippled plains and lions disappearing from underneath their roars, while the absence of bird-song in the trees made us look up for the first time in years.

When we woke to find the ocean shorelines lower by fifty feet, we knew the fish were gone: not only whales, dolphin, mackerel and shark, but trout and sunfish from the inland streams. This occurrence was accompanied by widespread repetition of the same dream, in which the dreamers imagined the ocean depths to be full of holes, like gigantic swirling nets that suddenly collapsed into bits of unconnected string.

But when the dogs shambled over hills and into alleys and did not return, the trouble began. Everyone started to walk on tiptoe, as though afraid the streets might break, and several began that curious habit, so prevalent among us now, of stepping to left or right every few feet, or suddenly hopping to one side as if avoiding a puddle, although nothing was in their path.

Finally, all the animals were gone, except the cats, and it was then we began to groom them like sacred plants, tend them like statues, as though they were our only connection with some remote, almost unimaginable past. The cats, for their part, continued licking their paws, purring, and prancing by us unconcernedly, acts which absorbed our interest for hours each day and endlessly fascinated the young. In fact, cat-watching became the favorite family activity, until we started to read of cat disappearances and cat carcasses found mutilated in ditches and alleys. Several cat owners admitted to the killings, then more and more came forward, each saying that his animal's remoteness had enraged him. And while all this was happening, couples in increasing numbers were discovered in charred bedrooms burned to death with their cats, as if they had enacted the end of some unspeakable love pact.

These incidents began a furor of cat killings, until so few remained that their rarity made them valuable commodities. Each day murders were committed to obtain one and ingenious thefts devised. In the end, for the people's good, governments, in international accord, outlawed the ownership of cats and collected and supposedly destroyed the ones that remained.

Now the few of us still owning cats are forced to hide them and to deny on official documents that they exist. Periodically, there are accusations at town meetings, and sometimes riots ensue, in which vigilante groups march from house to house by torchlight, searching for cats to shoot or burn and hang from lampposts for all to see.

Of course, we cat owners treat our cats with more tenderness than ever. We even keep them with us in our bedrooms, where, purring, they squat in corners bunched on their claws, the first images we see in the morning and the last ones we see at night, although many of us have awakened with a start in the early hours to see two silver disks blazing at the foot of the bed like the eyes of an idol about to come to life—two eyes blazing with the cold, unyielding light of the stars.

After the War

"It is absurd to resist what cannot be resisted," we said and hung the banners from every window. We did not know how arrogant the strangers would be. "Learn to accept the unacceptable and you will survive," they said, and began organizing us into labor gangs.

Their first decree announced that the avenues would not be finished, and we knew that all absences were permanent, that our hands were to remain open like the cisterns in the ruins beyond the city, where flies crawled back and forth on the dry clay.

In the manner of their speech, "absence" became the word we used to delineate those places where the avenues went unfinished, and "absence" also came to describe the ocean, where all roads end. The dog without a leash was no longer called "freedom" but "separation" and "rupture," for we now saw it tottering from garbage can to garbage can in the alleys, eaten by flies that fed on its mouth. Night, and the rooster who ended it, we simply called "sky," enunciating the firmament's changing hues with many synonyms, from "everlasting absence" and "cosmic separation" to "eternal rupture."

But soon we were faced with an unsettling incoherence: An old man, addressed by the new expression for "good morning," crumbled to dust. A widow, calling her son to supper in a recently revised phrase of endearment, was ripped apart by a pack of wild dogs. And during the last election, mobs of voters, thinking they were obeying the new voting instructions, crowed the names of their choices like drunken choirs as they jigged and curtsied around the polling places. After this incident—a situation the strangers would not tolerate—plans for future elections were canceled, and whole neighborhoods were trucked into the desert, never to be heard from again.

The new language was with us in our bedrooms and kitchens, as if it had been assigned to live with us for the duration, always foreign but always there, until each of us seemed to be occupied by a second self, or more accurately by two people, one whose presence we took for granted, and the other who we watched in terrified fascination, like a husband or wife you realize one day you have never really known.

The rubble piled up: scraps of old letters, broken plastic clocks, buttons and old batteries, rusting springs. War was imminent, the strangers announced, which was a surprise to most of us, since we thought that war was what we were engaged in already.

What would have happened had not the janitor discovered the armies encamped in the fields beyond the unfinished avenues is pure conjecture. But children were already stopping on the street and for no reason hauling down their britches and shouting words at passersby that no one could understand.

"Where are you going? Back to your homes!" blared the loudspeakers on the trucks. "There is nothing there: no army! no fields! Absence exists beyond the avenues! Absence, separation—only that!"

Some turned back, but most of the crowd continued on, and we heard the murmurs from the people in front spreading back to us like the sounds of a distant ocean, until all of us stood beyond the concrete pilings of the unfinished avenues, laughing, applauding, crying, and pointing at the field beyond, where the soldiers, whose uniforms we did not recognize and who did not notice us, seemed to caper as they went about their chores, singing the old songs of love and death in a dialect we recognized from before we were born, while their red, violet, and yellow caps bobbed in the sunlit breeze.

The Manual for Twentieth-Century Man
(and Woman)

This is the manual for twentieth-century man—and woman.

That field of flowering mustard, so brilliantly yellow against the darker green, is not what it seems. Atomic waste, buried miles beneath, provides it with that iridescent sheen.

If the sky is blue, it's raining two states over. If you love your wife (or husband), you must hate your mother (or father).

The woman with long blonde hair driving the car in front of yours is probably a boy on his way to a baseball game.

To be late for a lunch with friends is to miss the auto wreck that would have smashed you to steaks and chops. Or is it the other way around? You'll never know, unless you were on time for the auto wreck, in which case you missed a good lunch.

If you rise one morning with a sense of wonder and joy pulsing through your body all the way to your nerve ends, it could be a signal that a cancer has erupted in your colon or a black wen is budding on one of your lungs.

Something is always happening that you can't see. The worms are digesting the field. Mosquitos are hanging like tiny hams from the spider's tremulous rafters, while a squadron of bees, in Africa or Brazil, has begun the flight which will result in the end of the human race.

As you fold the laundry, finish your coffee, or read these words, keep in mind that hundreds of light years out in space, an asteroid, which will crash into our planet two thousand years from now, is about to be deflected from its original course by the last ripples of a starburst that occurred three billion years before our solar system was born...

O this is the manual for twentieth-century man, tra-la, twentieth-century man, tra-la. O this is the manual for twentieth-century man, tra-la, and the womanual for twentieth-century woman.

A New Kind of Surfboard

A man invented a new kind of surfboard.

Carrying his bedroom door down to the beach, he strolled through the shallows, slid the door flat on the swells beyond the breakers, and, hauling himself on top, stood unsteadily as a wave swept him into shore.

The surfers cheered. The man had added a new dimension to the sport, one that was easily attainable at any lumberyard, and that made surfing before his invention seem somehow incomplete.

True, surfing until then had been like skimming over the skin of the sea in a speedboat, and now resembled lumbering shoreward in a barge. But now there were so many possibilities: two or three surfers, even whole families, could ride one door, and several doors lashed together could make a raft on which acrobatics could be performed by half a dozen or more.

Soon people everywhere on the planet—paunchy fathers, middle-aged wives, sons and daughters—were carrying closet, living room, even bathroom doors down to the coastlines of the world. The oceans close to shore were speckled with doors, doors nudging through the swells, or sliding their flat-bottomed keels down the slopes of waves, in many cases fathers and daughters laughing and shrieking on them as if they were riding a roller coaster.

But doors are primarily doors in our minds, no matter how else we may think of them, and so a curious phenomenon occurred. While lying on their backs and staring at the sun on a day the waves were listless, a number of surfers imagined that the boards rolling against their spines were closed doors, and that they had just entered a room as big as the sky. If this was true, then the houses on shore were the ceiling and where horizon and ocean met was the floor, and not only was the world turned on its side, but if the surfers tried to rise and walk, they would fall through miles of air, as if they had stepped from an airplane in flight.

Those surfers lying on their sides, half-asleep in the sun, became aware that the shoulder resting on the door was actually holding it shut against the weight of the sea, and that the sea was pushing with greater insistence each moment on the other side. Some imagined hordes of skeletal dead swarming up through shadowy fathoms and battering against the door, and the surfers felt that at all costs they had to hold the doors shut.

And so, for different reasons, those lying on their backs and those lying on their sides refused to move, and soon the oceans were littered with humans clinging to swaying doors, doors sprinkling the oceans' surfaces like so much flotsam from sunken luxury liners.

Meanwhile, the people who remained on shore—wives, husbands, invalids, and those who are always left to do the laundry, wash the dishes, or prepare the meals—were calling from windows into alleys and backyards, or into other rooms, "The doors. What's happened to the doors?" From all the towns and cities that line the coasts, these words rose unanswered into the afternoon, such a hubbub of voices that neighborhood dogs joined them, baying and whining into the sky.

The doors, meanwhile, were tugged by the tides farther and farther out to sea. Still, nobody moved. Everyone was silent, flattened against the wood, clutching their boards.

What might have happened is anyone's guess. But the tides turned, as they always do, and slid the doors like triumphant armadas into all those separate shores, the surfers—couples, families, trios of friends—standing and cheering and waving to each other from their cumbersome boards, knowing they had not only endured, but had set the world right, so the sky was above and the land below, and the dead were wound in the shrouds of the sea once more.

The surfers were met by crowds of family and friends who in fear had come to look for them and now rejoiced at their approach, and with arms around one another they hurried to their homes, leaving the doors scattered on the sand like so many numberless dominoes staring blankly at the sky, although some of the surfers remained, standing wild-eyed alone or quietly in groups, as if waiting for something to happen.

The man who had first used a door as a surfboard had been trapped with the others. When he arrived on shore, he stood his door on end in the sand, and, joined by those surfers who had not gone home, made a circle of standing doors, just as people all over the planet would do in the nights to come. Then from the doors that still littered the beach, he built a fire in the center of the circle, and he and the others sat around it all night, watching the movement of the stars, not waiting for a sign or giving thanks, but observing, as if for the first time, that they lived in a mansion of endless rooms joined by invisible alcoves, vestibules, stairways and halls, all connected by an infinity of doors.

The Novel

Several characters in a famous novel moved to another town. They were tired of enacting the same old adulteries, fistfights, and successful marriages, and when they heard about a Tibetan guru living on the California coast, they went to learn from him the way to escape from life's miseries.

The characters who remained in the novel were outraged or confused. A number of them just stopped in the middle of a gesture or a conversation, refusing to budge from page 20 or 60 or 203, even though other characters kicked or slapped them, shouting words like, "Get up! Get up! We'll show them! They weren't that important anyway." Or, "I never liked Tom. He ruined chapter 5 with his arrogance." Or, "That Margaret. Did you see what she was wearing on page 179?"

Many of these remaining characters married, cheated, had affairs with, beat up or befriended the wives, children, brothers and secretaries of those who had abandoned the novel, in more than a few cases revealing desires and grudges that had never been suspected before.

All of these changes caused extraordinary alterations in the millions of copies of the novel that had been published in dozens of languages around the world. Pages where the characters who left had loved, dreamed and argued were now white spaces like unexplored territories on maps, which in a number of places the other characters would not, or could not, cross, and approached with scorn or trepidation.

The new marriages, arguments, and friendships expanded some chapters while shortening others, hopelessly confusing not only personalities but scenes as well, so that where two characters had previously strolled by shopfronts on a mild spring day in New York City, smiling and whispering and occasionally stopping to kiss, now one character was talking and gesturing to himself and turning a corner into the middle of a firefight in the jungles of Vietnam.

As a consequence of such realignments, the pages of the novel seemed to rearrange themselves. Page 203, for instance, traded places with page 51, pages 110 to 143 now followed page 275, and pages 310 to 327 wiggled their way into place between pages 15 and 16.

Readers could not adjust to all these transformations. A number of them suffered strokes or coronaries, their doctors ominously declaring that their hearts had attacked them. Other readers simply stopped functioning or began shouting at neighbors' wives, or throwing themselves sobbing into their brothers-in-law's arms.

The book company that had published the novel was overwhelmed by millions of lawsuits and, in an adroit legal maneuver, sued the author for breach of contract, claiming that the altered novel was not the one they had agreed to publish, or, indeed, *had* published.

In the end, the courts sent a delegation of eminent critics to approach the author and order him to rewrite the novel as it had originally appeared, or suffer the penalty of death, since he was responsible for the initial work that was causing such hardships for so many in its present form and, therefore, was clearly "a wicked, immoral, iniquitous and recreant act against the public's welfare."

On a hot sunny day, the delegation found the old novelist working in his garden, wrestling bushes and vines into a barrel, the creepers seeming to fight him off like inept tentacles.

"I was expecting you," he said, wiping the sweat from his face and neck with a towel. "But there's not much I can do. I created those characters all right; I won't deny that. But from the moment they woke on the page and I instructed them to say this and do that, they said and did whatever they wanted. I even warned them about their drinking, and entering that mine with rotting timbers in Arizona, but they never listened. I finally decided to leave them alone and just be here, in case they ever wanted to talk."

The head of the delegation waved the novelist's words away. "You know the consequences if you refuse?" he said.

The novelist shrugged. "I suspect those renegade characters will return. That may be the saddest thing of all. But you never know: all the characters have surprised me before, and there's no reason to think they won't surprise me again."

Journeys

Journeys

Everything we undertake is a journey. Frying an egg, sipping a beer at a party, or making a bank deposit, we are on a journey as great as the ones undertaken to Troy, Mecca, Mt. Meru, or to Cathay along the old Silk Road.

We slide the egg from the pan to the plate, sit down and eat, then go about our chores, which may involve a "real" journey downtown or even across the seas.

But each event *is* a journey, nonetheless: The egg is a volcano that might have happened on the plate's plateau, and a landscape unfolds on the table beyond the plate. Although we are seated, we are on a journey across this landscape of crockery and glass, calling out to someone seated on the other side of the continent, someone we hope is there, waiting or making his or her way toward us.

If the chair opposite is empty, there is still the person at the party who has made his way toward us through a human forest, or who we approach from the opposite direction through the same stand of talking trees.

We have debased so much. Consider the short trip across the teller's counter at the bank. Doesn't it resemble a confessional in church? The little gates are open, and the person on the other side is waiting to hear whatever you need to say.

Tourists

for Joe Stroud

In this land everything is poor. The people have pressed their backs into postures of humility and climb from crevices to beg for food.

We offered them coins, which they immediately ate, unaware of their teeth breaking. We offered them our scarves and hats, then our key chains, staring as they devoured each one.

Finally, we broke off slabs of rock, which some of them ate, while others began nibbling our pant legs or running their wet tongues along the sleeves of our jackets.

We fed them our words, whole sentences, paragraphs, but still they kept eating. And when we turned, we found they had devoured our car, which lay on its side like the skeleton of a cow.

It was after they ate our clothes that the slimmer of us were able to escape: we ran naked among them and began wrenching up roots and desperately chewing.

Later we remembered that our passports had been in our pockets, and the guards at the border have refused us permission to pass.

Now we squat at the edge of the snow, waiting for tourists. But when they arrive, they only throw coins. We want to tell them who we are, and when no one is looking we attempt to grab their hands, which they hurriedly withdraw.

We have not lost hope, but we grow hungrier every day, and each of us has admitted that he can detect the odor of tourists for hours before they arrive.

Cities

At 4 a.m., the only sound is the tumbling of the fountains in the piazzas everywhere in the city, their stone basins endlessly flushing and filling.

The fountains glint beneath the moon like open flowers.

Flowers everywhere in the city, then, and the city a gigantic flower incorporating the fountains and the piazzas into its design.

Historians and archaeologists say we built the cities for commerce, the marketplace. But at such hours as this, when the city lies open to the heavens like an intricate, man-made flower, I like to think our ancestors, obeying some half-understood impulse, were acknowledging our inclusion in a celestial ecology, as if, intuitively, they were trying to attract the tiny, buzzing stars.

In the City of Sunlight

I

When strolling through the cobblestone streets with their nickel–plated gutters, one cannot help but observe the play of sunlight so peculiar to this city. Not only does the sunlight flutter from the nickel and from the chrome edges of the window frames, but it butterflies from the domes, bell towers and bridges, all made of platinum or polished pewter, and especially from the silver bells, where it sprawls in patches until they boom out the hour. Then it takes wing above the rooftops, a migration of butterflies dipping and soaring, darting in and out of streets, and fragmenting into a thousand other butterflies when it carroms off a platinum statue or the platinum canopy of a fountain in one of the city's hundred plazas. At such times, if one is a man turning a corner, he may see at the end of a shadowy arcade, or directly in front of him, a woman he half-remembers in the act of turning away from him; and if one is a woman, she may encounter the slim–hipped man she has always dreamed of, pirouetting away from her like a ballet dancer.

Chalices full of jewels, glittering autos, glistening roasts—in short, anything wished for, anything desired (whether consciously or not) can be seen in the sunlight flittering from one metal object to the next. For these butterflies of sunlight are really butterflies of the imagination, and this is the city where dreams are made palpable for a moment and then vanish, only to reappear for an instant in another courtyard, another platinum-fountained square.

It is unlikely that the founders of the city intended these manifestations, since historically the city has been known for both its high incidence of suicide and its paucity of marriages. In truth, the city would have become a cemetery of silver–encrusted tombs centuries ago had not the youth of other nations made it a resort.

II

The young people come in spring, summer and early autumn, when the city brims with sunlight almost daily; and they come in great numbers, most of them arriving alone or with friends they quickly abandon; hardly ever with parents or in couples. This virtual migration has always been considered a curiosity when one remembers that no regularly scheduled airlines or ships serve the city, that only a weekly train visits it, that neither maps nor native guides can be found to direct one there, and that the city, actually a baroque ruin facing the ocean, is no longer inhabited. But that is why this city, with its crumbling walls overgrown with weeds, with its unkempt trees swaying ominously overhead, with its vines slithering everywhere, even onto the weed-cracked sidewalks, where piles of masonry are gathered at the base of buildings or clutter the nickelplated gutters—that is why this city is a city of the young.

III

During the tourist season, one can see the youths dashing through the streets, arms outstretched, the males growling, the females gasping, as they attempt to catch the elusive sunlit phantoms. This is how they spend their days, falling exhausted at dusk and sleeping until dawn when they resume the pursuit. Sometimes two youths, chasing the same flitter of sunlight, but from different directions, will run into each other's arms; and sometimes, eyes glazed, they will remain holding on to each other for months, even years, their lips curved in a secret smile. These are the lucky ones.

The majority continue to bound after every sunlit bauble, pulling bricks from walls or searching among the masonry piled in the streets or wherever the sunlight seems to vanish. Few of the youths want to leave at vacation's end. Many stay. Some go mad and run off into the jungle. Others sit in the city's many abandoned doorways, hands open in their laps, and stare straight ahead: the fluttering sunlight continues to reflect on their irises, but the irises no longer move. And some realize that the butterflies would all disappear if the sunlight could not flutter off the metal, and individually or in groups they set to work polishing the domes and the towers, so that the metal has remained polished throughout the centuries although the city has decayed. A few even recognize that the phantoms are only a reflection of sunlight, yet they cannot give up their pursuit and continue sprinting through the streets with increasingly haggard expressions.

IV

The rains usually end all this. Winter here is a continuing torrent of silver shafts, all spearing straight into the heart of the city, which accepts them like a martyr. In this season, the faces of the young, pale and unshaven, their hair like grimy rags, can be seen at windows, looking out at the glistening city.

How they die is not important: suicide, heartbreak, the body just giving up. All winter long, their parents, most journeying great distances, charter boats and planes, or struggle through the jungle on foot toward a location they do not know, yet somehow remember. And almost always they arrive too late. These parents, who had encouraged their children's trip and bade them farewell the year before with such joy as they could hardly understand, return home so distorted with grief that their neighbors cannot bear to look at them, for the grief seems a double grief, as if the parents had somehow left their own lives in that vine-strangled city.

Before returning home, however, the parents bury their children in the jungle, so that by spring, when the sunlight begins its explosions of wings from the belfries and the first of the tourists enter its streets, the city is empty and quiet and seems to have been waiting all year for the young people to arrive.

The Cult of the Burning Flowers

" . . . In the city's fortifications, there were quarters set aside for those selected to perform atonement for the populace. These penitents, both male and female, were chosen at random from among the citizenry without regard to age, and were housed in dormitories set above the huge inner courtyard just inside the western wall, the wall that faces the sea. This courtyard really an enclosed grass field, was exposed to afternoon sunlight and surrounded by palm trees whose fronds could be seen, rising above the fortress battlements, from the center of the city.

Each morning a priest, in a white robe and a headdress of flamingo feathers, entered the dormitories and announced the day's tasks. Ritual bathing was scheduled every two hours, beginning at sunrise and ending at 11 p.m. Ritual dressing occurred at 8, 12, 6, and 10. The hours between were assigned to long silences, fasts, scripture reading, slashing each other with knives, or poking at one another's skins with needles until each participant seemed covered with berries.

After a month of preparation, the acolytes, moaning hymns, would sway from the fortress, a procession of two hundred men and women in black robes, their heads shaved, and proceed through the crowds gathered on the boulevards, until they reached the palace garden, which the governor had made into a public park. Here, wearing an elaborate robe of peacock feathers and a silver-blue wig that fell in tiers to his shoulders, the governor would greet the acolytes in the name of the king. Then he would lead the procession, followed by the populace, back to the fortress, where the elders waited in the grassy courtyard, arranged in a circle around a pile of twigs, each holding aloft a burning torch and dressed in a scarlet robe open down the middle and a headdress topped with slender, sapphire-blue plumes that curled at the tips.

The acolytes would surround the elders, and then one of the elders, without a signal, would step onto the twigs inside the circle of his peers and lighting the twigs with his torch would be consumed in flames while standing erect, his torso so cleverly prepared over the years, through a continuous process of lancing and healing, that when his body blackened it would burst open and seem to gush forth a multitude of many-colored flowers before he fell.

The achievement of this effect was all-important, and was thought to manifest a favorable disposition of the gods toward the city for the coming month, at the end of which the next immolation would be performed. In time the penitents became known as 'The Cult of the Burning Flowers' and their acolytes as 'The Kindled Buds.' In fact, words describing acts of penitence and horticulture are so interchangeable in their language that they have caused scholars much confusion.

At first, the position of the dormitories made historians think that the fortress was a prison, since the quarters were located in the fortress and open to the sea breeze on one side and the huge sunlit courtyard on the other, both common architectural features found in our penal system today. But documents recently discovered make it clear that they were not prisons, since theft and homicide rarely occurred in the city, and that 'The Cult of the Burning Flowers' flourished with the people's consent and unswerving belief that those who sacrificed themselves were keeping a moral and spiritual balance in the universe that would benefit all living things and resurrect the dead.

Flowers were named for the martyrs, whose remains were buried on street corners throughout the city, and around whose graves small shaded parks were made and maintained by the populace, those same parks which lend the city its singular atmosphere, at once festive and pensive, that has drawn tourists to the town for uncounted years, especially during the last two weeks in April when the international horticultural convention is held. For two weeks festivities occur day and night, culminating on the final evening in the fortress's great inner courtyard, where the old men of the town, surrounded by their grandchildren, stumble in circles for hours on end, finally opening their shirts and tumbling forth a profusion of red and white camellias, just as they fall to the ground in a drunken swoon."

The Myth of History

My friends told me that poets should turn history into myth. The models they cited were Homer, Virgil and Milton, two of them blind, one a proper Roman. They found connections, my friends said, that make our sufferings and failing flesh worth the effort, and we emerge more robust for the moment, not cured of our sufferings and the tumult of our days, but grander than in our daily lives, where we shuffle through the years in rumpled clothes.

But I wasn't interested in myth. I wanted to call the broom in the corner what it was, and the old woman in the park, surrounded by shopping bags full of empty egg cartons, by name. I wanted to record as accurately as I could the terror of the boy the instant he scraped his knee on a pavement square, and the despair of the small dark man in Sacramento who came up to me, clutching the want ads, and said, "I guess my job is being out of work."

All I write about, however, are brooms that dance like awkward girls, and empty egg cartons that when opened are full of birds that chirp and fly into the sky.

I'll be frank: I distrusted mythic stories from the start, as if at an early age I realized that Homer and Milton couldn't see the world they lived in, and that Virgil told the unlikely tale of a man who carried his father from a burning town, and led his wife and son to a new and unexpected life where he became a king, although his wife and father died along the way.

Soon, however, I determined that history was lacking too. There had to be more than the boy, the instant his knee hit the pavement square, being as terrified as the son who held his father's hand amid the screams and flames of that ancient town; more than the unemployed man in Sacramento being equally forlorn as the father who led his family from their burning home and wandered aimlessly for years.

Wives and fathers die, and bills still have to be paid, and there's little hope of being rewarded with a decent job, let alone a crown. What remain are those flocks of birds that burst into the sky from non-existent eggs, and brooms that lurch around the room like adolescent girls behind their window shades.

I don't know much and understand less, but I'm aware that such images as these have flitted through our minds from one age to the next, without our knowing where they come from or what they mean. Instinctively, however, I sense that those tottering brooms do not so much recall a restless goddess locked inside a tree as the wild sap leaping through trunk and branch on windy nights to shake itself free from its imprisonment in wood, just as widows and old men, hobbling around their solitary rooms, would wrench themselves out of their skins, if they could.

Anyone Writing an Epic Today

Anyone writing an epic today wouldn't use those phrases that were the epic's stock in trade. The verbiage would be reduced from "Gerald, the golden spear-wielder," "James, the bowman, bright in bronze," or "Harold, chariot handler, who led the men of Akron from their fortress-favored hill" to "Jerry, the tennis pro," "James, the cop," and

> Harry, the used car dealer from Akron, who came from that
>   smoggy city
> With three Chevrolets loaded with passed-out cousins he guaranteed
> Would be cleaned up and ready for combat the following day...

And there would be less about preparations, about the gatherings and sortings, the assignments of battalions to this ship or that, and the stowing of shields and supplies in trucks and cargo planes before the journey got underway.

Some contemporary writers might dispense altogether with that sun-bright morning when the hundreds of black ships set sail for the East, or the six thousand tanks and trucks revved their engines all at once in a convoy more than a mile long, and the exhaust fumes rose above the plain like a gray rag that covered the sun and the blue heights of the cloudless sky.

Anyone who wrote an epic today would be aware that journeys do not begin, but only continue. And after the peerless heights of Ilium or Detroit lay in ruins, smoldering behind the ships departing for home, ships crammed with shifting mounds of jewels and fatherless daughters bruised and weeping in their rolling holds, the journey would not have ended, but merely gone in another direction. And those survivors—who escaped in underground passages, carrying fathers and holy scrolls—would already be planning future chapters no poet, in his blindness or second sight, could surmise.

Only the motivations would remain the same, and the reactions of the victors and the vanquished, and the future rising like a gray rag high over whiskey-yellow plains into the steep blue of the receding sky, and even of that no one would be certain.

And no one would be certain if the one who understood—the shrewd tactician, visionary, saint; inventor of wooden horses or Ghost Dance shirts—would find his way home years later, only to discover that home was no longer there, and may never have been, that wife and son were gone forever, and that the Ithaca or Akron he had dreamt about for so long was only an island or oasis harboring a fire-scorched cairn, a stopover where he could rest for a week or a year before he had to pack up and wander on.

The Truth of the Matter

The problem with truth is that although it seems incontrovertible, without alternatives, each of us has his or her own truth, which makes a lie of everyone else's. At the same time, it is true that the truth erases all sorts of pressures, such as guilt and anxiety. Those who lie, however, must conceal their falsehoods by hanging a smile on lips that would rather tremble, or by raising an eyebrow over an eye that would rather look away, until the face becomes a stage on which the features perform a popular play everyone knows because of what happened to its author. He was the one who committed suicide rather than reveal the name of the Revolution's leader to his country's secret police.

You remember the play, I'm sure. It begins with the lover, pistol in hand, entering through the French doors at the rear of the stage and hiding behind the sofa. The husband enters stage left, and the wife stage right. The husband cannot see the lover, but the wife can. The lover has not expected the wife to be there, and knows she will not approve of his plan to kill the husband. To disguise his intentions, the lover leaps up, aiming the pistol at the husband, and demands that he open the safe behind the portrait of his first wife, which hangs above the fireplace, stage left, where crimson ribbons, blown by a table fan offstage, flutter in the grate. The husband refuses to open the safe, the wife screams, and the lover fires the pistol, killing the husband.

The wife continues to scream and the lover, frantic that the servants will hear, shoots her. Dying in the lover's arms, the wife tells him that she screamed hoping to stop him from killing the husband because earlier that evening the husband had told her that the lover, who he thought was merely a neighborhood acquaintance of hers, was his son by his first wife, the one whose portrait hangs over the fireplace with the false flames. On one knee, clutching the wife's body to his chest, the lover slumps in tears, and delivers a long monologue in which he says he will love the dead woman until the end of time and will pay penance for killing her and his now-revealed father by joining the Revolution.

During the lover's monologue, the old family butler has entered stage left. Overhearing the stricken young man's last words, he informs him in a shaky voice that his master was indeed the youth's father, but he was also the secret head of the Revolution for whom the secret police have been searching for years. The butler then implores the lover to take the money in the safe behind the portrait of his mother to the headquarters of the revolutionaries. While he speaks, the butler hobbles to the portrait, pushes it aside, twirls the combination of the safe behind it, and hands the bundles inside to the bewildered lover, telling him the revolutionaries' address as he shoves him out the French doors, which he locks behind him.

Alone, the old butler delivers a short, grief-stricken speech in which he wonders at the tragic ironies of life and tells the audience that the dead man was really *his* faithful butler and that *he*, the supposed butler, is the husband of the woman in the portrait, the lover's father, and the secret head of the Revolution. He had become a revolutionary, he explains, following the death of his first wife, the woman in the portrait, after her lover attempted to murder him but whom he had luckily killed instead, along with his wife, whom, although she had plotted his death with her lover, he has loved to this day.

The butler is interrupted by loud banging and shouting offstage. He identifies the tumult as the secret police, and picking up the pistol the lover has dropped near the wife's body, he announces that he is the author of the play and will kill himself rather than tell the authorities the name of the head of the Revolution. He shoots himself in the heart just as a civilian and four men in uniform rush into the room stage left.

The civilian is the lover. He is carrying the bundles of money from the safe. He stands over the butler's body and tells the four uniformed men that he is the head of the secret police and has been posing as the lover of the dead woman on the floor; that, in fact, he is the son of the lover of the woman whose portrait hangs over the fireplace, and has dedicated his life to finding out what had happened in this room the night his father was murdered so many years ago. He was still a babe then, he says, in the arms of the deluded peasant woman, his mother, who, as the four uniformed men know, started the Revolution because her husband, his father, had betrayed her with the woman in the portrait, the wife of the aristocrat who owned this mansion and had treated the peasants with such cruelty.

The four men in uniform exit with the three bodies. After they depart, the lover looks around to see if anyone is watching, then strides to the safe, redeposits the bundles, covers the safe once more with the portrait, and stands looking up at the picture, while the crimson ribbons flutter in the fireplace at his feet. After several moments, the lover begins to speak to the portrait in a quiet voice. He curses his duplicity as head of the secret police, mourns the death of the butler and the master, declares undying love for the master's second wife, and pledges allegiance to the Revolution—all because of what has happened in this room during the last hour. Then he picks up the pistol which the fallen butler had dropped on the carpet, and slowly walks toward the French doors at the rear of the stage.

At that moment, someone shouts from the audience that he is the head of the secret police and the lover is to stop where he is because he is under arrest and rifles are aimed at him from all over the theater. In a panic, the lover whirls left and right, lifts the pistol to his head, shouts that he is the playwright and will not reveal his leader's name, and shoots himself just as a dozen uniformed men, armed with submachine guns, rush onto the stage.

As the uniformed men stand looking down at the lover's body, the audience leaps to its feet as one and applauding wildly begins to sing the revolutionaries' forbidden anthem. The audience is an army, two thousand voices strong, which pushes towards the exits singing, until the theater is empty.

The voices can be heard receding in the streets outside, amid the sounds of gunshots and breaking glass. On the stage of the empty theater, two of the men in uniform help the lover to his feet. The three of them are laughing softly and talking in low, indistinct voices, as if in a crowd scene in a play. Several others, having sat down on the sofa, are lighting cigarettes. Standing near the fireplace, staring at the still fluttering ribbons, one of the uniformed men asks the lover if it will be safe to go home through the streets. The lover shrugs, but the old butler, who has come on stage with his jacket off and shirt unbuttoned, says that, as always, the safest place is where they are, and advises everyone to spend the night in the theater because by morning, he exclaims, his voice rising dramatically and his forefinger pointing skyward, "The city will be ours!" At this pronouncement, all the men on stage, including the butler, break into laughter.

When the laughter has died down, the same uniformed man who asked if the streets were safe, a boy, really, who has recently joined the company, nods to the crimson ribbons in the fireplace, and asks how the prop manager conceived of simulating fire so ingeniously. "Simulate indeed!" replies the butler. "I wouldn't put my hand in it if I were you," and, with the others joining in behind him, he breaks into louder laughter than before.

The 8th, 9th, and 10th Wonders of the World

In the midst of a civil war, two men were arrested in different sections of the same city and summarily sentenced to be executed the next morning.

One of the men had been a spy and blown up a barracks, killing twenty soldiers. The other had done nothing, but his protestations of innocence had gone unheeded by his captors.

Both men spent their last night in the same cell. The cell, which had been the basement of a family home before the war, smelled of urine and goats. It contained no lights and no furniture, and the two men sat in the dark on the straw-strewn stone floor, exchanging small talk about their lives and listening to the howitzers thumping on the hills above the city and the small arms fire occasionally stuttering through the streets.

Suddenly the spy blurted out with a bitter laugh, "They say there are seven wonders of the world—the hanging gardens at Babylon, the lighthouse at Pharos, the great wall of China. But they are all things men have built, physical things, and almost every one of them has disappeared like dust in the wind, as we will tomorrow.

"I tell you this: there is an eighth wonder, my friend, and it is the human imagination. We can conceive of anything—not just those seven constructions, but a warm willing woman who will love us when we are lonely, a good meal when we are hungry, and the successful end to this war, when we will finally be at peace and our people in power.

"That is what keeps me going and is why I blew up the barracks—and that is why I am not afraid to die."

His voice shivered away in the darkness.

The innocent man shifted on the straw but didn't reply. His face was covered with shadows and the spy could not see his expression.

They sat in silence for several minutes when the innocent man began to speak with great difficulty in a small voice, as if he were struggling to find the words for his thoughts. "I don't know. I was thinking as you spoke that there had to be something beyond the imagination. I'm not sure, but maybe it is the fact that somewhere along the line those who have taken me from my wife and children and condemned me to die will be forgiven.

"If I cannot forgive them, maybe my wife will, or my children, or my children's children. I mean, hatred cannot go on forever.

"And when it occurred to me just now that all of us contain this capacity to forgive, I said to myself, 'If the imagination is the eighth wonder of the world, surely forgiveness is the ninth.'"

"I'll agree to that," exclaimed the spy with a snicker, "if you agree that the tenth wonder is our capacity to forget."

The Canary Islands

"What islands are those?" I asked the first mate.

We had passed several treeless, rolling islands, wind-ruffled yellow under the pale blue sky, each without houses or any sign of human habitation.

"The Canaries," he replied, unshaven, his black sweater grimy at collar and cuff.

"All that wheat," I said. "Who plants it?"

"Those are the canaries," he said again. "Hundreds of thousands of them fly here several times a year and bunch together on the swells."

I had taken passage on the only ship available during that hellish war, a Yugoslav tanker, all rust and shuddering metal. I never knew its cargo: the crew sneered whenever I approached.

"You can't be serious," I said to the first mate, still staring at the island. He didn't reply, but spit on the deck near my shoes, and lumbered away.

I leaned on the railing, peering at the landfalls. They certainly could have been birds, birds who sought refuge from the world's murderousness, flying from everywhere on the planet at appointed times to huddle together and be revitalized.

The next day they were gone, and I didn't ask about them again. But I still imagine them, those temporary islands, suddenly coming apart in the night, separating into hundreds of thousands of wings scattering to the seven continents, where they fall like pieces of moonlight on the houses of the sleepers, silent, unseen, neither substance nor shadow, yet more than a possibility, a presence, really, that periodically departs from our lives but always returns.

The Man Who Committed Suicide

Every evening the man would climb to his room high above the city and read the newspaper.

Even though he was weary from his work as copyreader, he was horrified by what he read—children abducted, tortured and sexually maimed, religious sects hacking off one another's arms and legs with axes, nationalist groups either bombing orphanages and hospitals or being bombed themselves.

The man's wife had died the year before. His children were grown and, like his few friends, had moved to another city. There was no one to whom he could express, as he wrote on a note pad, his "immense disgust at the barbarity of the human race."

The night he wrote those words, he swallowed a bottle of sleeping pills and went to bed for the last time.

However, he woke the next morning surprisingly energetic and filled with a sense of well-being. Outside his window, the sunlight snapped like the peach-colored sails of an immense clipper ship.

He was, he had to admit, glad that the supposedly lethal dose of sleeping pills had not worked, and when he set off for his office, he almost bounded down the stairs.

But outside, the streets were silent. The news seller slept in his stall, automobiles dozed at the curbs. No one was on the street. One block after another was empty and the man could hear nothing but the wind slapping the buildings and his footsteps, as if frightened by the silence, following close behind him.

He hadn't gone more then two streets from his apartment when he understood that all the people were sleeping in the buildings around him, as if they had taken the sleeping pills, and that in all the city he was the only one awake.

He wandered through the city all day, stared at the still ships in the harbor, listened to the different tonalities of wind sailing down the boulevards or beating on the walls of tall buildings.

That evening there were no newspapers and the news seller sat as he had that morning, open-mouthed and snoring.

The man climbed to his room and sat all night at the kitchen table, listening to the wind.

Next morning there was the same wind-warped silence, and the man had walked half a block past the snoring news seller before he realized what he had to do.

He returned to the newsstand and for a moment stood before the snoring old man with his two-day growth of beard and his five tobacco-brown teeth showing behind his slack lips.

Then the man leaned forward and kissed the news seller on the mouth, a kiss that was gentle and firm at the same time.

The news seller came awake instantly, saying, "What? What?"

But the man had already turned from him and didn't reply when the news seller, confused by the empty silence, called after him.

Readying himself for the task ahead, the man increased his pace, knowing there were several million sleepers in the city.

The Word That Wanted to Change
Its Meaning

There was a word that wanted to change its meaning, but no matter how hard it tried it couldn't take off its clothes.

Truth is, words don't wear clothes. They think they do, and no one is sure of where they got such a notion.

But who wants to argue with words? Who'd dare to, since you need other words for your argument, and they just might rebel, switching sides in mid-argument out of a sense of loyalty to their own kind, and causing all sorts of mayhem, like laying siege to the King's English.

Anyway, the word that wanted to change its meaning was determined to undergo that transformation. The politicians had used it one way, and the church fathers another, and the businessmen had used it anyway they wanted, until the word no longer knew who it was, and was determined to change its life.

"Freedom! Liberty!" the word proclaimed, but they were both on a lunch break in a small café on a side street in Paris, discussing the identity crisis both were undergoing at that moment.

The word, meanwhile, sat down in the middle of the street, and after pouring a can of gasoline over its head, held a match aloft and prepared to strike it. "That won't change anything," said a passing student. "If you're called black instead of white, you'll just be a dead color charred beyond recognition."

Just then, a cop dashed over and said to the word, "Okay, you, you're blocking traffic," and when the word didn't budge, the cop took the ticket book from his back pocket and demanded, "What's your name?"

The word didn't reply. Not that it was disobeying the Law, but since it wanted to go by a different name, one that it hadn't found yet, there was no way it could answer.

"So you're gonna play dumb," the cop said. "Well, I'm gonna run you in." And he grabbed the word by one of its meanings and took it to the police station.

"Any aliases?" the desk sergeant asked in a bored voice.

"Of course not," the word said, more frustrated than angry.

"You're in contempt for refusing to answer to your name," said the judge, banging his gavel. "30 days."

Now the word was getting angry. After all, it hadn't done anything, and here it was on its way to the county jail.

"You're number 33, 333," the prison photographer said, putting a block of stenciled numbers in front of the word's chest.

"I'm not a number! I'm a word!" said the word, so they sent it to the penitentiary, stamping its file INCORRIGIBLE.

"You've got the wrong word," the word yelled when it read the name on the file, and the warden locked it in solitary.

The state psychiatrist was no help. "A normal word accepts its place. You can't deny who you are: it's sociopathic behavior," he said.

"I refuse to accept this sentence!" said the word at this point, which was what everyone had feared, because the sentence fell apart, and then the paragraph. In an instant, the word vanished from conversations, causing embarrassing, sometimes confusing incidents, as well as riots from Calcutta to London. Simultaneously, the word disappeared wherever it was printed. Whole pages collapsed everywhere on the planet, while all the books in libraries fell on their sides, as if their spines could no longer hold them up.

Now some of you out there think this is just plain silly. Others, amused, are reading to see how it will end. A few detect nuances and verbal shadings that suggest deeper meanings, while several are reading between the lines, which, of course, is empty space. But the majority of you are thinking, "What's the point?" And here, if I wanted, I could ease your displeasure by calling up those old moral saws, "No word is an island," or "Do not ask for whom the word tells, it tells for thee," but that would be too easy.

Suffice it to say, that because of the catastrophic situation the word was causing, the government put it in the witness protection program, knowing it would refuse to testify on its own behalf, and sent it to live somewhere in Idaho under an assumed name that—you guessed it—the word refused to accept. The government reasoned that since the word was now out of circulation and keeping its mouth shut, the crisis would soon disappear. And it did.

As for the word, living in such an overwhelming solitude, it eventually redefined itself, and one night stole away from its anonymous life. Nobody knows its new name, or where it has gone. The FBI, however, has put it on its most wanted list, citing its antisocial tendencies. The Bureau is afraid that if the word turns up in its new meaning but its original identity is recognized, it could cause mass schizophrenia among the populace.

The powers-that-be concur. They fear what would happen should a new strain of the word break out among us to which we were not immune. As the bipartisan committee charged with investigating the situation said in its final report, "There are no known vaccines to counteract the possible effects that mutations of the word might engender."

Laughter

The man who laughs in the company of others is close to a knowledge he won't admit, like someone in the midst of a fusillade of sneezes, coughs or hiccups. His eyes water and shut, his hand on the revolver loosens and shakes, while the other hand reaches for the back of the chair to hold him up.

I don't care who he is—beggar or jailer, banker or auctioneer—if he is laughing with others while they laugh, he is part of a club whose members must allow themselves to be helpless in the presence of others, since he is acknowledging, for that moment at least, his helplessness at being helpless.

Even if the focus of his laughter is a boy with electrodes attached to his penis and a crown of spikes around his head, or a ten-year-old girl lying spread-eagled and whimpering in a circle of laughing men, the one who laughs with others has made himself vulnerable in a way that the man who laughs alone has not.

Don't misunderstand me, please: I excuse no one. I just think it is best for us to laugh together, no matter what the circumstance, for then there is always the hope that one of us will become embarrassed at his behavior in front of the others and say, "Enough!" and will unhook the boy and cover the girl with his coat.

I think this because I have come to view Creation as an eruption of solitary laughter that was all mouth and starbits and molten gases spewing out of eternal loneliness, a laugh literally laughing at nothing, for no reason, a laugh that is still going on and will continue to go on as it has, until someone steps forward to change the metaphor and calls out "Enough!"

The Ultimate Place of Exile

Whenever I find myself about to knock people's hats off in the street or to shake my fist against the night, I think of going into exile.

Siberia, with its white winds swirling over the brittle tundra, or the Antarctic, with its glinting hills of chilly silence, are too civilized.

What I'm looking for is the most remote, the ultimate place of exile. I deserve nothing less.

At about this point I remember my elbows, those barren peninsulas jutting out into the universe, the most ignored parts of our bodies.

They are as far from our thoughts as Australia and Timbuktu, and Easter Island and Tierra del Fuego aren't nearly as remote.

Nor does it make a difference if we choose one elbow or the other, since both are equally desolate.

Neither tropical nor arctic, jungle nor desert, the elbows are continents of calcified waste rarely visited by sun or moon but almost always covered with fog as dense as wool or thin as cotton.

They are the place of continual solitude, where nothing happens until they whack a door knob or a table-end, and, more shocked than surprised, we howl like a sleeping dog awakened by sirens. In fact, only on those occasions do we remember that our elbows exist at all.

Yes, I conclude, the elbows are the ultimate place of exile.

Then a strange thing happens. Like a shipwrecked sailor who explores the rocky island where he wakes, once I become aware of my elbows they occupy all my thoughts.

As if for the first time, I realize they are promontories of bone hinging our upper and lower arms, so our hands can reach and our arms embrace.

They are also like two skulls, as if God had run out of parts in making us and, having to improvise, had capped those hinges with the cranial coverings of infants who had died the day they were born.

At the same time, He had the sensitivity to place the elbows where we could not see them, and kept them from our thoughts until those moments when we needed to remember they were there.

And what is there to remember except those unlived lives that were attached to our own so we could touch and embrace others who were equally alive and reaching out to us?

I mean, is there any act more affectionate, more gentle, than reaching for and holding the one you love by the elbows? Notice the gasp at first, or the shudder, at the unexpectedness of it, and then the softening of the other person's body, as if you had touched the secret place where hardness ends and vulnerability begins.

When I reach this thought, I am ready to come back into the world. I am ready to return from my exile.

Lost Things

Those little things we search for, find us—the misplaced key we unexplainably notice as we pass the kitchen table for the fifth or sixth time; the watch left in a pocket that days later reappears still ticking on a mantel or a windowsill, with arms raised in mock surrender at five of one.

Even our dead parents seek us out in sleep, and those love affairs, which ended so badly, search for us in pop tunes on car radios late at night, or in photographs which weren't there yesterday but this morning unaccountably appear in our bureau drawers.

There are some things, however, that fall so far inside us they cannot return without our help, like children in a tropical rain forest after an airliner crash who must wait for us to undertake an expedition to rescue them.

Harnessed in cumbersome backpacks and strapped into oxygen tanks made of steel plates stippled with rivet heads like nineteenth-century ship hulls, we forge into the jungle from the clapboard river town.

Soon our equipment litters the path behind us and we stagger on, gasping, barefoot, clothes shredded, as if pulled toward a destination we cannot resist.

Each day we are more frantic because time is running ahead of us and we fear that we'll never catch up.

In the end we find the children seated blank-eyed in a clearing or in a thatched hut, pounding husks with stones. They have grown so tall, so thin, their faces as gaunt and weary as our own, that we hardly recognize them.

Later we stand by the graves we have discovered in the underbrush. They are wild and overgrown, no longer visited by anyone and strewn with what the survivors identify as religious artifacts—keys, watches, combs, and yellowing photographs of us.

The Light Was Out

I kissed her in the hallway. The light was out. She didn't love me, and I didn't love her. We fumbled with each other in the darkness at the bottom of the stairs, and our breath was more like hissing than lovers' murmurings. I thought it then, and wasn't half surprised when she broke away and stood shuddering in the shadows, turned from me. "No," she said, "they'll hear." She'd said that the other time, and the time before that, when the light was on, and I imagined them, old and in bathrobes, coming to the stairhead, looking down on us and calling, "Ellie, is that you?" But now the light was out and there was no excuse. "Come on," I said, and reached for her because I thought I should, although I knew it was no use. "No!" It was as final as goodbye, and was.

I never saw her after that, but heard from time to time that she had married and divorced and married once again, that she had a daughter by her first husband and a son by the second. She would be fifty-six or fifty-seven now. I remember her saying that her parents were old and wouldn't understand, that her mother was forty when she had her, and her father over fifty. I thought they were her grandparents when I met them.

She was fifteen or sixteen that winter, and I a year or so older. But I can't help thinking that she's older than her parents now, since they've remained the same age in my head as they were then. Is she too old to understand when her own children giggle and fumble in the dark at the bottom of the stairs? Does she remember, when she hears them whispering, the night we faced each other in a similar darkness, unable to express anything but confusion and self-protective anger, and went our separate ways without so much as a goodbye?

She didn't love me, and I didn't love her, and the light was out at the bottom of the stairs. She came into my arms only to push me away, a woman about to leave her girlhood and a man who was still a boy, both too young to know we were her parents then as we are her children now, as we stood face to face on the darkened threshold.

The Field

I loved to lie in the grass when I was a boy. I'd lie on my back, looking up through the tree branches as the sky flew away in its blue and white robes.

But mostly I'd lie on my stomach, peering through the forests of grass. Soon the ants would arrive, or a beetle on his way to somewhere else.

The longer I lay still, the more birds and animals would appear and the more I would feel less like myself and more like the field, an expanse where bees and robins settled for a moment before flying on.

Now I sense rustlings and quiverings everywhere around me, as if tribes from the same valley were getting ready for a journey. The tree branches resemble a spider web in which I am caught, or the sky is, and when I turn over the ants are already there, and behind them the beetles picking their way over stones.

There are moments I can hear the weeds unfurling their wings and the grass sliding upward, nudging aside acorns and leaves.

At such times I think this is all I can hope for. Not that the plants or animals have come to greet me, but that they don't even know I am there.

Wristwatches

I

When I was a boy the only responsibility I understood was winding the watch my father gave me when I was ten.

If I forgot to wind it, time would stop: streetcars and pedestrians halt in their tracks; cityscapes and countrysides become hard and still as those scenes stencilled on porcelain dinner plates.

Each day I grew nervous and sweaty as the hour drew near for me to wind the watch. What if I forgot at the last moment? What if I didn't wind the watch enough and the next day contained only twenty-three hours, so the spinster mathematics teacher didn't get enough sleep and was irritable in class, or the President, exhausted, made the wrong decision, causing massive unemployment or plunging the nation into war.

What if I overwound the watch and everything speeded up, as in an old movie: rushing cars, waving arms and stiff-legged steps trying to keep up with time, or to "catch the moment," as my father would always advise: "Learn to catch the moment when it's offered, son, or force it open when it's not."

I replaced the Stations of the Cross with the twelve apostles of the watch. To each one I murmured hymns of praise or prayers of contrition, so the day would advance. Each apostle was a soloist deferring from his pedestal to the next one in line, as the short-armed magician touched his wand to the following minute like a conductor directing a symphony orchestra.

For months I wound the watch daily at the same hour and wore it strapped to my wrist like a medal. I don't know when this obsession would have ended had I not unaccountably lost the watch. I still remember how panic shot through me when I realized the watch was gone, but also the relief I felt when—to my astonishment and, I must admit, considerable irritation—time did not stop.

II

When you retire in my country, the company you work for presents you with a watch. This is a decidedly vicious act, suggesting that you are supposed to spend the rest of your days observing your final years ticking away, or at least be constantly reminded of your approaching death by the presence of the new watch.

By the time I retired, I had learned that I could never catch the moment but only run after it like a child chasing a hoop down the street, although recently I have thought that each of our lives was the moment—not enclosed by the moment, mind you, but the moment itself crammed to bursting or partially filled, like an attic or garage where we store old furniture, clothing, and photo albums. Each moment is random and bumps into other moments and sometimes holds a fellow moment in a kind of magnetic fascination, until both merge into a third moment that continues bobbing and rolling and bumping its way through crowds of celestial bric-a-brac, while mama and papa wave good-bye in the distance.

III

I now suspect that each watch takes the pulse of its wearer and determines the exact number of moments allotted to him, rationing its stored energy accordingly, as if inside the watch a woodsman were chopping down a tiny forest, one tree at a time.

Beyond this forest is a land of intersecting lines of light. The light, like luminous threads, slides along fractures and edges, defining linear hillsides and airy corridors. We are inside one of the corridors which slowly turns in circles around us while at the same time leading forward. The corridor walls are transparent and we can see all the way to the darkness surrounding us, or, since the walls take on a mirror-like sheen against the night, we can see ourselves reflected in them by readjusting our gaze. These walls are cut in jagged, skewed angles and balanced on end like fun house mirrors or a succession of razor-sharp guillotines.

We follow the corridor to the end where it opens onto an arena. Spectators, dressed in shimmering silver or storms of color-changing reds and golds, buzz and hum in the stands above us, chatting in a language we cannot understand. They are so busy quarreling or muttering, in fact, that we are not at all sure they have come to see us do whatever it is we are supposed to do—balance a plate on our nose while standing on one foot, race a sweaty giant, or battle each other with swords and tridents: everything that human history, it seems, had been training us to do in the hope that when the time came we would be ready to face what—with a reverence that in retrospect has to be considered laughable—our parents and grandparents referred to as "the future."

Another Myth for the Millennium

It is dark. There is a point of light in the forest. It is a very old forest, where the trees lean together and howl like chained women when the wind thrashes through them, the wind like a fat man trying to escape from a dream of women tearing at his clothes, holding onto his lapels and pockets so he can't get away. He is so slick with sweat that his clothes slide everywhere over his body. Already his flesh is gouged, his face slashed. If only he can reach that point of light he can see through the brittle arms and pawing hands.

This is a recurring dream that begins and ends with this scene whenever the fat man falls asleep, and he is positive he is recalling the penultimate scene of a former life or the future of the one he is living.

To avoid this dream, the fat man stays late at the office, where he devises mergers and contracts with hidden clauses, commands armies to march, and makes up crossword puzzles which contain the words for everything except his name. Each of these diversions is an afterthought he immediately forgets, but each is tinged with his terror of falling asleep.

Despite his precautions, the fat man knows that eventually he will have to sleep and will find himself once again in the midst of the forest, being ripped and lashed by the howling trees. And once again he will yearn for that point of light, not knowing that it comes from one of two places: a cottage where an old woman goes about her chores, muttering his name over and over again; or a bonfire where a band of thieves makes plans to rob him, listening with hissing teeth to an old man with a smoke-white mustache whose corporation the fat man has acquired in a hostile takeover.

Even when the fat man isn't there, the chained trees howl and thrash their arms. They howl for lost sons and kidnapped daughters, wanting to grab generals, businessmen and politicians, and demand explanations before tearing them apart.

In the cottage, the old woman putters in one room or another, no longer able to remember if she is muttering the name of a dead husband or a lover who has abandoned her. Deeper in the forest, shadows of firelight flicker like war paint over the faces of the thieves, all laid-off workers from the fat man's factories. They listen with bared teeth to their mustached leader who quivers with words of revenge and thoughts of growing fat once more with businesses and power.

I'm convinced that this dream was perpetually dreamed from each of these points of view, one after another, and that when the dream was dreamt from all those perspectives at once, it erupted in the darkness like a helium-filled balloon, and our universe was born.

And when the dream is dreamt simultaneously from all those perspectives again, our universe, like that same balloon, will shrivel to a point of light and become one of the many stars we see each night, all of them other dreams that have been tried and have failed.

The Stone Flowers

for Donna

There was a time when stones flowered. I need to believe that. In forests and fields, layers of black rock cracked open after rain, and slick pink petals swarmed into the wet sunlight. And those who saw this weren't astonished because such blossomings happened all the time.

As recently as the nineteenth century, miners reported seeing chunks of coal blossom with blue flowers as tenuous as flames. Some said walls of coal sprouted blue flowers all around them, and with picks at their sides they stood speechless at the wonder of it.

On the beach at night, I've seen the sand shimmer with a green phosphorescence. The next day I imagined the sand was acres of seeds, and I thought, "That's what this Earth is: seeds."

And when I look up at the stars sometimes, I think that's what this planet is, a seed hurtling with others through space.

When my wife weeps for our son or the death of a relative, I think of all the seeds scattered over the earth like unlit points of light lying gray and dull next to golden specks of mica and the glassed-in worlds of opal with their trapped swirls of celestial flame.

I know that the earth is full of cinders and hard seeds that have never blossomed, and that it makes no difference if pink flowers once surged from layers of black rock, or if one day the planet will crack open and shoot a pink and blue geyser into the night that will unfurl like a celestial flower.

I know that whether times are good or bad, we ride this planet like mites crawling on a pebble.

That is why I am not ashamed to say that flowers once blossomed from stone: I need to believe in every possibility. We all do.